FITNESS
on the go

*The anytime anywhere holistic workout
for busy people*

FITNESS
on the go

*The anytime anywhere holistic workout
for busy people*

ABHISHEK SHARMA

RANDOM HOUSE INDIA

Published by Random House India in 2012

1

Copyright © Abhishek Sharma 2012
Abhishek's exercise photographs by Pia Sukanya
All other photographs by Abhishek Sharma

Random House Publishers India Private Limited
Windsor IT Park, 7th Floor, Tower-B,
A-1, Sector-125, Noida-201301, UP

Random House Group Limited
20 Vauxhall Bridge Road
London SW1V 2SA
United Kingdom

978 81 8400 193 8

Typeset in Minion by Eleven Arts

Printed and bound in India by Replika Press Private Limited

Dedicated, in all humility, to my fitness teachers
R.C. Sood, Premamay Biswas, and the late Jernail Singh

Before You Start

Before following any advice or practice suggested in this book, it is recommended that you consult your doctor regarding its suitability, especially if you suffer from any health problems or special conditions. The publishers, the author, or the photographer cannot accept responsibility for any injuries or damage incurred as a result of following the exercises in this book.

Contents

Foreword

Coming from a sports family and being an athlete myself, I understand the importance of being fit and healthy. Before I started acting, I used to play competitive badminton, and was used to going through rigorous physical training. When I started working in films, I missed my regular workouts and desperately felt the need to workout to keep physically and mentally fit. An actor's life is extremely hectic. There is no fixed routine, and fitting in a workout—or rather being regular with one's regimen—is not the easiest thing to do.

That's when I found Abhishek. Abhishek's training and fitness philosophy makes it easy to include exercise in my hectic and irregular day-to-day schedule. His combination of yoga and freehand athletic workouts is fantastic for busy people like me, and keeps you in shape in a very effective and holistic way. I've been training with Abhishek for the past three years and it has made a huge difference to my fitness, wellness, and energy levels. I am almost addicted to it now! It has become a part of my life and routine.

Abhishek's training programme is motivating because he changes my routine according to my needs on that particular day, and comes up with a new, innovative workout each time. At the end of my workout, I feel fit, my mind is calm and focused, and I don't feel exhausted. Instead I feel fresh and ready to meet the challenges of the day ahead.

When I have a very hectic schedule and have no time for an elaborate one-hour workout, I still try to squeeze in a short workout with him. Even a 20-minute workout with Abhishek makes a huge difference to my energy levels and productivity through the day.

When I am travelling, I keep up the running, Suryanamaskars, and the wake-up stretches he's talked about in this book.

His approach to holistic fitness has made a huge difference to my life and has helped me explore my full potential. I am so glad he is sharing his holistic workout through this book so that busy people like you can benefit from it, like I have.

Deepika Padukone
April, 2012

Introduction

Busy people

There are two kinds of people who usually seek my advice on fitness. There are those who have been following some kind of fitness routine and have enough time and energy to invest in an elaborate four-times-a-week workout routine.

Then there are those who have woken up to the fact that they need to start doing something about their fitness before it's too late, but have genuinely very little time in their day to invest in a comprehensive workout, or to join a regular fitness class.

This book is particularly aimed at the second group of busy people who urgently need to exercise and genuinely want to, but who either don't know where to start or how to go about addressing their deteriorating fitness due to time constraints.

The last time many of these people did a workout or played a sport was probably back in school or college. Once upon a time, they may have been very active physically, but it's been a while!

In a desperate attempt, many of them sign up for a gym membership but are unable to attend once their initial enthusiasm dies down. Worse still, they somehow manage to get themselves to the gym, or do some other kind of high-intensity fitness workout for a brief period of time and then either stop abruptly or injure themselves—sometimes leaving their bodies in a much worse state than when they began.

If you're one of these busy people, it's not that there is no hope for you or that you should not even try. You just need to be smart and well informed and do the right kind of exercise that best suits your needs. You also need to modify your day-to-day lifestyle without delay, making it more active and healthy.

It is possible for a busy person to get really fit, even with a minimum investment of time. No matter how little time you have, I am determined to help you take charge of your holistic fitness.

We live in a time of constant technological innovation and so-called advancement, but along with that, there often comes a decrease in physical activity and an onslaught of unhealthy repetitive movement. Aside from this, we are tempted to consume more processed foods with unhealthy side effects, so it is now absolutely necessary that we make a conscious and sustained effort to restore and maintain our health, fitness, and well-being.

About the book

In this book, I have shown you a way to achieve all-round and holistic fitness. It's not about fads, shortcuts, or some new clever way of exercising, which promise results without any effort. Shortcuts are short-lived. My approach to fitness relies on age-old wisdom and natural ways to getting fit, which have stood the test of time and have long-term results. The movements in the exercises are natural and my lifestyle advice is in sync with nature instead of trying to outsmart it with fancy gadgets.

By 'all-round', I mean we will be working towards all aspects of holistic fitness and concentrating equally on strength, flexibility, stamina, balance, improving posture, breathing, and mind centring. Just playing a sport, or only strength training in the gym, or just yoga practice does not cover all these aspects of fitness in totality.

Along with athletic freehand exercises like push-ups, squats, running, and brisk walking, I have included a lot of elements of yoga in the exercise routines. Yoga practice helps to relax the mind, soothe the nerves, enhance breathing, improve posture, create a balance at every level in the body, and initiate healing. In the fast-paced world that we live in, it is important to follow a healing practice like yoga or tai chi to counterbalance the ill effects of a modern lifestyle on our health and well-being.

Having trained in yoga—the traditional, classical way—I do believe that the ultimate purpose, method of practising, and the benefits derived from the yoga postures are very different from other fitness exercises. Being the busy people that you are, you might not be able to make the time required for yoga postures, so I have incorporated them within the workout routines so that you do not lose out on their immense health benefits. Moreover, as a beginner, being warmed up and sweating in a workout will help you perfect the yoga postures faster and more easily. The postures have been used in a way that they blend into the exercise routines without losing their essence.

A lot of holistic knowledge about health and fitness might not have had extensive scientific research, but nevertheless, holds true. Walking barefoot on grass makes you feel nice and is good for you. Period. I have been doing my own research, by way of my own practise and in the course of training people, to arrive at the methodology I have given in the book. All that I talk about here is based on my experience, on first-hand proof that it works, on myself, and on the people I have trained over the years.

For the past ten years, I've been constantly working on evolving a complete holistic fitness practice suited to busy city people, based on my own training in martial arts, sports, and yoga. I now call this practice *Victory Yoga*. It is a practice suited to the modern day *Arjuna*—the everyday warrior who has goals to achieve and challenges to face.

In *Victory Yoga*, I draw only those elements from athletic fitness training, martial arts conditioning, and yoga practice that are most relevant to busy people.

People like Deepika Padukone, Ranbir Kapoor, and Sonam Kapoor, among many others whom I have had the privilege to train, epitomize the hard-working, goal-oriented busy people that this practice is meant for. My endeavour through my sessions is to help my students and clients be fit, centred and achieve their true potential.

In this book, I have further simplified the practice to suit even the busiest people, who can't take out even an hour three times a week, which is generally the amount of time I expect my clients and students to invest in workout sessions.

The workouts I have described can be done anywhere without any equipment. The routines consist of natural freehand movements primarily using one's own body weight for strength exercises and the available natural surroundings for other exercises. Such freehand exercises like brisk walk, jogging, push-ups, squats, and yoga postures have long-lasting results. They make the body proportional, strengthen core muscles, improve posture, and build an athletic physique.

Throughout the book, I have also explained the basics of fitness in simple terms. These are important to know to be able to devise your own workouts, choose what is best for you, modify your routines, and avoid making mistakes that can do more harm than good to your health and fitness.

Whether you are starting from scratch, or after a long gap, you will learn how to start in the right way, according to your present capacity, and create a workout routine suitable for you. Even if you have been working out, and are leading a healthy lifestyle, this book will help you to evolve your workouts further, understand the basics of holistic fitness, and clarify a lot of common misconceptions.

This freehand workout will go beyond just making you slim or muscular. It will improve your functional fitness, the ability to do your day-to-day activities, as well as any physically demanding activity, with great efficiency and effortlessness. Instead of just cosmetic muscle building for show, it will help you build an athletic physique, which is attractive as well as capable enough to enable you to trek, climb mountains, play a sport, run a marathon, simply play an outdoor game with kids, or run up the stairs effortlessly.

Apart from improving your fitness, the book will help you adopt a healthy and holistic lifestyle. The emphasis, throughout the book, is on living in harmony with nature, as much as possible, even while leading an urban lifestyle. The workout described is holistic, incorporating breathing exercises, yoga postures, as well as a proper freehand athletic workout which you can continue evolving and practising even with advancing years. In fact, you will never feel old if you follow the exercises and lifestyle changes that I have described and make them a part of not just what you do, but who you are.

How to use this book

The chapters in the book are devised progressively, with each chapter preparing you for the next. To get the best results, it is important to go through each chapter without skipping forward.

I have used many terms like *cardio, functional fitness,* and *freehand exercises* in the book. Important definitions like these are explained at the end of Chapter 2.

Chapters 1 and 2 are about incorporating healthy lifestyle changes and clarifying facts and myths on various aspects of fitness. You will have fun going through the twenty 'Healthy Habits' to see how many of them you are following already. Incorporating even a few that you are not yet following will make a huge positive change in your life, even before you begin any exercise!

The exercise routine in the second section of Chapter 3 will make you aware of your fitness strengths and weaknesses.

In Chapter 4, you will be preparing your body with a 'One-Month Commitment'. This preparation will lead you to 'Incorporate Six Fitness Gems', including the Suryanamaskar, in Chapter 5. Equipped with the six gems from Chapter 5, you will begin the 'Basic Workout' in Chapter 6.

Then in Chapter 7, you will learn how to take charge of your own workouts and how to adapt them to suit your own specific goals.

In Chapter 8, you will get a glimpse of Deepika Padukone's workout routine.

The adoption of Chapter 5's six fitness gems is a milestone in itself. By reaching there, you would have already made an excellent return on your time investment of a 'One-Month Commitment' in Chapter 4. It is very important to prepare your body by taking the four weeks in Chapter 4 to perfect techniques of important yoga postures and freehand exercises which will lead you to the six gems. If you sincerely follow the book to the point of incorporating the fitness gems in Chapter 5, you would have made a huge difference to your fitness already. If you wish, you can even continue to practise the six gems for another month or more before you move on to Chapter 6, the workout chapter.

I cannot stress this enough: Don't be tempted to skip the 'One-Month Commitment' in Chapter 4 just because it appears to be long and seemingly easy in terms of the exercises I'm asking you to do. This is because when one is starting afresh, or after a long gap, the body needs to be gently introduced to exercise with progressive increase in intensity before moving on to any high-intensity workout. If you are quite fit already and have been exercising regularly, then you can shorten the one month commitment by doing just one session from the exercise routine given for the first week, and then move on to doing the next session from the routine given for the second week and so on. This way it will take you much less than a month to get through this section, yet you will not be missing the flow of exercise progression that I have designed for you.

A word about technique. A detailed description of each exercise is given the first time you come across that particular exercise in the book. This is another reason you should go through all the sections step by step so that you are familiar with the exercises explained in the earlier chapters. The second time the same exercise is mentioned, the full description of technique is not repeated, so if you need to refresh, simply refer back to the description of its technique. The page number will be mentioned to help you quickly flip back to the instruction. The 'Basic Warm-up' is described in detail in Chapter 3. The same warm-up will be used to prepare for the exercise routines in later chapters, with variations only for the cardio part of the warm-up.

If you want to write to me with specific questions about anything in the book, you may do so at: abhishek@victoryoga.com

Ease In

Fitness Checklist

Ask yourself a few basic questions:

1. Can you touch your toes without bending your knees?
2. Can you climb up seven flights of stairs comfortably without getting unreasonably out of breath?
3. Can you do around ten push-ups effortlessly?
4. Do you feel fit enough to play football with kids or go on a trek right now?
5. Can you use an Indian-style loo with ease?
6. Are you near your ideal weight?
7. Do you feel good about your body when you see yourself in the mirror without clothes?
8. Does your spine arch back well?
9. Can you sit still comfortably for two minutes with your eyes closed?

10. When you sit on the floor, can you get up gracefully, without too much difficulty and without the support of your hands?
11. Do you have good posture and grace in your movements?
12. Do you feel energetic?
13. Do you breathe deeply?
14. Are you able to rest and sleep well whenever you want?

Are you achieving your full potential?

If your answer to most or even many of these questions is 'no', following the holistic workout in this book will turn most if not all responses into a resounding 'yes'!

The Promise

Even if you're too busy to take out enough time for an elaborate workout, or are able to absorb only a small percentage of this book, if you go on this journey with me with commitment, sincerity, and perseverance, I assure you it will immeasurably change your life for the better. I am not offering you any shortcuts; there are none. Buying into fads and shortcuts will waste your time, will do more harm than good, and might ultimately discourage you.

The path that I'm suggesting is a natural and holistic one. It does require effort, hard work and commitment from you, especially in the beginning.

Apart from becoming fitter and healthier, making holistic fitness an integral part of your life will bring a few more returns on your time investment and commitment:

1. You'll start losing weight, becoming leaner and slimmer.
2. Consequently, you'll feel lighter, and as a result, better.
3. You'll start to feel stronger, fitter.
4. And you'll feel your energy levels rise.
5. You'll also experience your stamina and concentration getting heightened.
6. You'll realize your functional fitness is improving, enhancing any performance, including love-making!
7. Your reflexes and balance will improve tremendously; making you ready for anything that comes your way.
8. As a result, your productivity will increase, which basically means, you'll get better at whatever you do.
9. You'll begin to look taller, the secret to which being your improved posture.
10. Your lung capacity will increase, which, in turn, will make you breathe better.
11. So naturally, you'll start becoming a calmer person.
12. As a direct result, you'll be warding off a host of diseases that all of us living a modern lifestyle are not only prone to but are inevitably heading towards as a result of our toxic and sedentary lifestyles.
13. You'll soon notice an improvement in your general sense of peace and well-being.
14. All of which will lead you to have that glow only truly fit people have, making you more attractive, successful, and happy.

There are some people you'll see who seem to have overflowing reserves of energy and exude a natural glow. Chances are that they lead a healthy lifestyle which undoubtedly includes a small personal exercise routine to keep their body and mind fit and healthy. It could be 20 minutes of yoga every morning, a walk, a run, or a sport. They have found what suits them and works for their fitness and wellness.

Even as you get older, it is entirely possible to have a fit and healthy body, and to explore your true potential.

As I write this, the three people that I personally know and look up to, who come to my mind instantly, are actor Anil Kapoor—my teacher and one of the greatest cultural ambassadors of India—Dr Karan Singh, and Viji Venkatesh who has been doing tremendous work for the welfare of cancer patients. These people may not be very young but can put anyone half their age to shame in terms of how productive and full of energy they are and how they look.

While Viji swears by her early morning walks and breathing exercises, Dr Karan Singh religiously starts his day with a short exercise routine for the body followed by his prayers and deep breathing to centre his mind. I was sitting with Anil Kapoor in a coffee shop during the making of his film, *Gandhi, My Father* of which I was a part as the holistic trainer for the main cast and crew. A fan came up to him complimenting him on his young looks and telling him how lucky he was to look like that at his age. Once the person left, Anil told me that perhaps many people don't realize how much effort he puts into staying healthy and fit by following a regular exercise routine and strictly watching what he eats to look the way he does.

You must find your own personal routine and keep evolving it according to your body, requirements, and life goals. In the following chapters, I'll help you devise a customized exercise routine and guide you in making some vital and wonderful healthy lifestyle changes. These are essential for you to lead a more complete and fulfilling life.

Healthy Habits

Before we begin preparing for a workout, I want you to go through twenty, extremely important yet simple healthy habits I have shortlisted.

Each one of these can make a huge positive difference to your quality of life and well-being. Try to include whatever you can from this list right away. To start with, even if you are able to follow just ten of these, you are on your way to being super-healthy.

Your Morning Routine

Stretch, like animals do, when you wake up

Observe a cat, a dog, or any other animal. The first thing they do when they wake up is stretch. That's what nature intended us to do, and no, not towards our mobile phone to put the alarm on snooze! Just a few stretches, with a particular focus on stretching the spine, will make a huge difference to your energy levels, alertness, and reflexes through the day.

Take a few deep breaths

Do this right after your stretches. They will keep you calm, relaxed, and ready to take on the challenges that will inevitably be thrown your way through the day. Also, remember to take a few deep breaths, especially when there is fresh air, through the course of the day.

While taking deep breaths, pay attention to stretching the exhalation much longer to empty the lungs fully before you breathe in. Just focusing on inhaling deeply with poor exhalation will be like focusing on filing a glass with fresh water when you have not yet emptied it of its earlier contents completely.

Drink water as soon as you wake up

Initially, one glass of room temperature or slightly warm water is fine. You can gradually increase it to half a litre and then to one litre according to your capacity. This starts a cleansing process in the body and will make you feel rejuvenated.

Keep water by your bedside when you sleep. When you wake up you can immediately have a few sips before moving on to wake-up stretches and deep breathing, then drink some more water after the stretches.

This simple habit will make a huge difference to your health, well-being, and energy levels.

Eat a few soaked almonds

After stretching, breathing exercises, and drinking water, eat a few almonds soaked from the night before. Four are good to start with. You can increase it to around seven in a few weeks.

Soaking almonds overnight makes them easier to digest and absorb their rich nutrients. Almonds are a great source of protein, Vitamin E, and calcium, among a host of other nutrients.

Soaked almonds are ideal to eat in the morning. The body doesn't digest them either too quickly or too slowly, but just at the right pace for an empty stomach in the morning.

If instead, as people often do, we eat something which is very easy to digest and releases energy quickly—like biscuits or jam and toast with tea—it raises the blood-sugar levels in the body too quickly. At the same time, eating something too heavy to digest first thing in the morning slows you down. I can't imagine eating a paratha first thing in the morning and then heading out for a run or yoga practice.

In the morning, our blood-sugar levels are low. Eating soaked almonds stabilizes these levels and releases energy slowly. It's a great way to start your digestive process. If you don't eat something soon after waking up, your digestive system doesn't get a chance to get activated in the right, healthy way. Not eating for a long time after waking up also causes acidity, which may lead to ulceration. Eating healthy soon after waking kick-starts the metabolism on the right note. A good metabolism is your key to better health and weight control.

Eat your favourite seasonal fruit

After the almonds you should have a fruit while juggling your newspaper and morning routine. Try to eat the fruit whole, with its skin whenever possible. Don't eat cut fruit that has been lying out for too long as it gets oxidized and loses a lot of its nutritional value.

While almonds will release energy slowly, the fruit will give you energy faster, providing you with enough for your morning exercise. Eating the fruit in the morning while your stomach is empty also helps the body to absorb its nutrients well.

Eat a full breakfast

Preferably after some exercise, you should have a good breakfast, within two to three hours of waking up. It's always good to take a bath before a heavy meal than immediately after, as bathing increases the overall blood circulation which otherwise needs to get directed to the stomach to aid digestion. Moreover, in the Indian ayurvedic tradition, it is believed that the agni, or digestive fire in the stomach, should preferably be on the higher side when you need to digest a heavy meal. This digestive fire gets mand or diluted by a bath, making digestion sluggish and inefficient.

Whoever said 'eat breakfast like a king, lunch like a prince, and dinner like a pauper' was right. A wholesome breakfast will keep you healthy and your weight in control. Variety is key—eggs or boiled sprouts and milk as protein, oats or dalia (made from broken wheat) as carbohydrates, and vitamins from milk and fruits. Make your breakfast a filling meal full of fresh, nutritious, and wholesome foods to kick-start your metabolism.

Through the Day

Take the stairs

Just doing a one-hour workout in the day is not enough. You must be active through the day. Walk around. Take the stairs instead of the lift. Park the car some distance away so that you can walk to the office. Take your dog for a walk whenever you can. Trot around the house doing chores at a fast pace. In short, find reasons and ways to walk and move instead of finding ways not to!

Move every two hours

So you workout every morning and even take the stairs whenever you get a chance, but that's no excuse to sit in one place for hours at a stretch while you work, browse the Internet, watch television, or do anything else leading you to inactivity. When you sit in the same position for too long your blood circulation and metabolism slow down considerably and the muscles start getting stiff, weak, and prone to injury.

The internal functions of the body are at work even while you are sitting at your desk for hours. Even while you are inactive, toxins are being produced in the body, as energy is being released in your cells. The body will only be able to flush out these toxins if you move often. Moving around at regular intervals helps the lymphatic system rid the body of toxins, prevents your back and other muscles from going stiff, and keeps your metabolic rate from slowing down. Helping your lymphatic system work well for you leaves you feeling more energized, fit, and healthy. And an improved metabolic rate helps in weight control.

Make a habit of moving at least every two hours. If you've been sitting for too long in front of your computer, get up, move around, and come back again. If you are on a long flight or drive, take a break in between to get up and walk around a bit before sitting down again. Get up and walk out during the interval of a long Hindi movie and try not to come back with too many unhealthy snacks!

Keep your back straight

Keeping an upright posture will help you stay in shape, make your core muscles stronger, and burn more calories. Wherever we sit—on our comfortable chair, bed, car, or flight—we mostly make use of the back support available, which doesn't help in making our core muscles strong. In the rare case when we do sit without back support, we tend to slouch, as our back muscles are weak due to excessive use of back support. Slouching is bad for our spine and the shape of our body.

When you sit erect, imagine there is a thread tied to the top of your head, which has a small hydrogen balloon at the other end gently pulling your spine upwards. Keep this image in mind, and it will help you get your posture right. My students find this really helpful. You don't have to schedule a special time to practise this. Do it anytime, all the time. If you're sitting on a

Good posture.   Bad posture.

chair in a meeting or watching TV sitting on the bed, sit erect without support for as long as possible—1, 5, or 10 minutes. Then switch to taking back support when tired. You might have to change the position of your computer or television and elevate them in order to practise sitting upright.

Practise this once in a while through the day. Try to increase the time duration to be able to sit straight comfortably without back support. You'll be burning calories, becoming stronger, improving the state of your spine, and getting a host of other benefits by just sitting right.

Also make sure your spine is erect when you're walking or even just standing.

Eat local, natural, seasonal, organic

Nature intended you to eat more locally grown, seasonal food. By local, I mean natural foods that grow around where you live, not apples from Washington! Drinking a lot of coconut water in Rajasthan might not be a good idea, but it is in Mumbai, where coconuts grow.

By natural, I mean fruits, salad, nuts, coconut water, whole grains, the most pure and least-tampered-with eggs, milk, chicken, and fish. Not necessarily foods which say '100 percent natural' but come in packets in departmental stores.

Be wary of vendors who proudly tell you that everything is available all year round. As much as possible you should eat according to the season: root vegetables and leafy vegetables in winter, watermelon in summer...you get the idea.

What to snack on

Try to throw in small meals—a bowl of fruits, some nuts, or sprouts—between the three big meals. Come up with your own creative recipes but make sure they are not highly processed, sugary, oily, or made from white flour. I find salad made from boiled sprouts great as an evening snack as it is filling yet healthy.

When you're out and about, try to carry a fruit, almonds, dates, or a fresh home-made snack with you so you don't have to eat whatever is available if you feel hungry. And if you have to eat out, try to avoid highly processed carbohydrates like biscuits or white bread; opt for whole grain bread or a salad instead.

Fifteen minutes of direct sunlight a day

Most of us in India have an obsession with trying to stay out of the sun to remain fair! But I can't stress enough how important direct sunlight is for us. Sunlight has immense life force or prana. Sunlight is the best source of Vitamin D, which helps absorb calcium from the food you eat, making your bones stronger. Fifteen minutes of exposure to sunlight is the minimum absolute must. Spend a good amount of time in the sun. However, don't overdo it either, especially if you are not used to it. As far as possible, try and soak up some early morning sun. It is less harsh.

Drink enough water in the day

I come across so many people who do not drink enough water during the course of the day. Water flushes out toxins and keeps your weight in check. If you feel a headache creeping up, or if you start to feel stressed out, try drinking a glass of water. Often, these symptoms crop up because of dehydration. If you are not used to drinking enough water then start slowly and build it up to drinking at least 2 to 3 litres of water a day. Before you eat a meal, if you're feeling thirsty, drink a few sips of water but not too much. After finishing your meal, wait for at least half an hour or forty-five minutes before drinking water. This aids the digestion process instead of obstructing it. Drinking substantial amount of water during or immediately after a meal dilutes the digestive juices of the stomach, thus hampering proper digestion.

Raise your heart rate for twenty minutes

Engage in sustained cardiovascular activity like running, cycling, brisk walking, stair climbing, skipping, or a combination of these to raise your heart rate for at least twenty minutes, preferably every day, or at least three to four times a week. This sustained activity, which is different from the short spurts of other activity throughout your day, raises your metabolic rate significantly. You'll feel the benefits of this for the next several hours, burning what you eat more efficiently, which is essential if you are to have a fit and healthy body.

Commune with nature

Find ways to keep in touch with nature. Grow plants. Tend a garden. Develop a relationship with an animal; befriend a stray dog. Breathe some fresh air. Soak in the morning sunlight when you get a chance. Spend time in greenery. Contact with nature is very soothing and healing. It's a great stress buster. Once in a while, look up at the blue sky and the stars. Walk barefoot on grass or sand and you'll feel the benefits instantly.

Cut out white sugar and processed, packaged foods

White sugar is in many things we don't think about. It's in cakes, mithais and even so-called 'healthy' biscuits; in colas and carton fruit juices too. White flour or maida is a refined carbohydrate, which on entering the body, gets easily converted into sugar. Avoid white rice, bread, processed food, fried food, and packet food as much as you can. Not only are they stripped of nutrients and high in ready-to-be-absorbed calories, the preservatives used in them are harmful to our health. Just remember, mostly, if it comes in a packet it's been processed and is not good for you.

Eat a balanced diet

Eat a balanced diet containing proteins, carbohydrates, fat, vitamins, minerals, fibre, and sufficient water on a daily basis. Don't avoid any taste completely. There are six basic tastes—sweet, sour, salty, bitter, pungent, and astringent. Try and include all these tastes in the foods that you eat on a daily basis.

Another simple and fun way to make sure that you are getting all the different nutrients is by including a variety of colours in your day-to-day diet—tomatoes, carrots, honey, green vegetables and salads, lemon, lauki or daal, milk, curd, paneer, or almonds.

If we avoid any particular food on a long-term basis, it causes a deficiency. Deficiency leads to disease, so balance is a must.

Winding Down

Do not sleep immediately after eating a big meal

Lying down immediately after eating a big meal will affect the quality of your sleep as well as the absorption of nutrients from the food eaten. Good-quality sleep should ideally provide much-needed rest to all organs and systems in the body including the digestive system. Sleeping immediately after a meal won't give that much-needed rest to the digestive system. Moreover, the heavy activity of the digestive system won't let you get good sleep, preventing you from feeling well rested.

Have an early dinner, as soon as possible after sunset. Try and sleep only after a gap of two to three hours after dinner. After dinner, sit straight or do something that requires you to sit straight.

Meditate. Pray. Relax. And breathe, once again

A car engine cannot be kept on continuously can it? Even our computers start to complain if we don't switch them off for days. Similarly, our bodies need to be switched off every day. How do we switch ourselves off? The best way is by some form of meditation—prayer, breathing, or relaxation—in which we surrender ourselves. There must be a point every day where we are not attempting to be in control of ourselves, where we let go and allow our internal batteries to be recharged instead of being continuously depleted. This mind centring and relaxation practice increases our awareness, our sixth sense, and our intuition. This also has a great healing effect on the body and mind.

Get around eight hours of sleep

Don't worry too much about what is the exact amount the experts think you need. We all have slightly different requirements which vary with age. Find out for yourself how many hours of sleep make you wake up fresh and full of energy. On the other hand, make sure you don't overdo the sleep either.

Don't overstimulate your mind before bed by drinking tea or coffee, watching television, reading, or listening to such music that will make your mind more restless. Choose to read or listen to music that makes your mind calmer. Give yourself time to wind down. Try to increase your quality of sleep by writing down the things you feel you need to remember to do the next day and then put it away. Wear loose and comfortable clothes. Wash your feet. Say a little prayer to help you relax and calm your mind.

As much as possible, sleep in complete darkness. If there is significant light coming in from outside, then draw your curtains. The darker it is, the more efficiently your pineal gland will be able to produce a hormone called melatonin which is extremely important for your health and well-being.

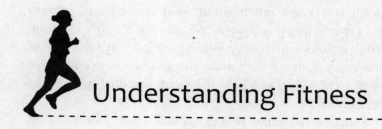

Understanding Fitness

Avoid Five Common Mistakes

I often come across people, especially those who have not been exercising for a while, making the same mistakes when they start working out. I am sharing these with you at the beginning so you can learn from the mistakes of others and avoid these pitfalls.

Take up exercise that's right for you—not what's the latest fad. Don't waste your precious workout time doing exercises that are not suited to you and which might do more harm than good.

Avoid an 'Outside-In' Approach

Workouts focused on acquiring a six-pack or muscles popping out of your T-shirt might not be for you, unless you are Salman Khan!

Avoid the common 'outside-in' approach to fitness. If you're particularly pressed for time and are not already fit, trying to sculpt your body by excessive weight training is like trying to focus the little time you have towards decorating your house from the outside before fixing the leaking roof through which water is seeping onto your bed! Become aware about the basics of fitness. Decide what your realistic fitness goals should be. Keep in mind what is good for you in the long run before blindly signing up for a gym membership, or buying that abs machine with the goal of sculpting your body to look like your favourite model's or film star's.

Instead, adopt the 'inside-out' holistic approach to both fitness and wellness. By 'inside-out', I mean get acquainted with the current state of your body, its strengths and weaknesses, correct its imbalances, and get your basic overall fitness in place. If you are obese or have a chronic back problem or high blood pressure or extreme stiffness or weakness of certain muscles or any such imbalance, when you decide to take charge of your health, you should prioritize fixing these first before moving on to other superficial fitness goals.

The right way to start is with holistic exercises like yoga postures and walking, and then moving on to freehand fitness exercises like jogging, push-ups, and freehand weights.

A lot of men who come to train with me have done a brief duration of body building exercises using machines and had to stop due to injury or lack of time. Their body is in a worse state than before. It has become stiff, disproportionate, injury prone, and weak. Training towards getting a bodybuilder's physique and training towards developing an athletic physique requires very different kinds of training. A bodybuilder mainly trains different muscles in isolation, working out different body parts on different days, whereas an athlete does more freehand exercises that work several muscles at the same time. An athlete works out all the muscles, works on all-round fitness, and doesn't ignore flexibility and stamina.

Professional bodybuilders, most models, and action stars build and maintain a muscular physique that requires them to put in a lot of time, energy, and effort. A bodybuilder's training is very meticulously supervised and very regular. And the truth is that they put themselves through huge discomfort to build and maintain their physiques. It is important to understand that sculpting a physique like a bodybuilder does not necessarily have much to do with fitness. Bodybuilders train primarily to show off their muscles—muscles that might not be of much practical use and prone to injury if not accompanied by enough stretching. Moreover, if you do this kind of training for a short while and then stop, it will be harmful to the body, leaving it stiff and injury prone.

On the other hand—athletic bodies, acquired mainly by freehand exercises, are truly fit and of much more practical use, as athletes train for performance. They pay a lot of attention to their core muscles, which are not even visible!

So you have to ask yourself: why you would invest your time—which you could devote to work, family, and other worthy pursuits—in getting a body which is just good to show off and is not of much practical use.

In spite of being aware of the pitfalls, if you still want to sculpt a bodybuilder's physique then go about achieving it like Salman Khan. He is a good example of a fit person. Salman was into sports and had a very fit, lean, and athletic physique to start with. He started bodybuilding at a later stage, and continued freehand and cardiovascular endurance exercises along with the heavy weight training. I had the opportunity to do a yoga-based stretching session with him. He has retained good flexibility in spite of his muscular physique. Moreover, he does a lot of cycling and brisk walking to keep up his stamina.

So even if you really wish to take up bodybuilding, first work towards getting truly fit and athletic—acquiring a strong foundation before you dive into it.

Avoid 'sprinting', especially at the start

When you start to exercise after a long gap it is very important to begin at a gentle pace and gradually prepare your body over a few weeks for a full-fledged workout.

People who've played sports or worked out at a high intensity in the past have a tendency to push themselves too hard when they are starting afresh after a long gap. If you have been a champion sprinter in your early years, and after giving it up have not been working out at all, it doesn't mean you can sprint on your first day or even your first week. In fact, it is best if you avoid a very high-intensity workout for a month, during which time the body needs to be gradually reintroduced to that kind of movement, the muscles warmed and woken up.

It might seem that I'm asking you to be too patient, but I see so many people, specially the ones who have done high-intensity activities like sports, martial arts, etc in the past, getting injured by pushing themselves too far too soon.

Just because you used to do 50 push-ups at a go years back doesn't mean you should start with even 15 if you have not been exercising for years. Perhaps you will manage 15, but why risk an injury? Start with 5 and gradually increase it so you can slowly get back up to 50 within three months. Also, make sure to warm up, specially if you are over 25, as it reduces the chances of injury.

If you are planning on a martial arts class, wall climbing, playing squash or football, or any such vigorous activity, try to make sure you prepare yourself for a few days beforehand. Walk, jog, and stretch so that your body is somewhat ready for the assault and doesn't get shocked. Otherwise, you're going to be seriously increasing your chances of injury.

Over the weekend, I get the people I train to do a long run outdoors or play a sport—often basketball. A friend of mine who used to train with me a few years back has been keen on joining in for a game of basketball with us as she was a fantastic player fifteen years ago. I've not let her join knowing that she might injure herself. Except for walking, she's not been working out for some time now, and just walking doesn't prepare you for an activity as vigorous as basketball.

You have to be jogging and regularly stretching before attempting such high-intensity activity.

Also you must warm up well before starting. In case you've had injuries or have a weak back or knees, then it's all the more important to start easy and make sure to do a warm-up before doing a strenuous activity like playing a sport.

I warn people I start training that the only thing that can stop them from getting super fit and in super shape is being foolish and getting injured. Sloppy technique or doing a movement with a jerk or without warming up or overstraining without proper technique can get you injured in no time. Which means you'll have to rest until you're healed, which, in turn, means you'll have to start from scratch again.

Avoid overtraining

Another very common mistake I witness time and again is people exercising at very high intensity without giving adequate rest to the body.

High-intensity exercise, though great for the body if done systematically and combined with right amounts of rest and nutrition, can get addictive and harm the body in the long run if not combined with adequate rest.

When we push the body too hard in a workout, it goes into repair mode. A vigorous workout followed by adequate rest and nutrition makes the body stronger than before. If the body is repeatedly pushed into high-intensity workouts while it is still in repair mode, it causes fatigue, lowers immunity, causes injury and, over a period of time, even permanent damage to our joints.

Though it might not apply as much to people who do not have much time for a workout, I advise people who want to work out every day that they should push the body on alternate days and do a lighter exercise, yoga, or mainly stretching on other days while the body is still recuperating from the high-intensity workout. However, if your daily exercise regimen is low intensity like a brisk walk and gentle yoga postures, you do not need a rest day in between unless you've pushed yourself too much on a particular day.

Be careful about overtraining—that is, not letting the body recuperate from the last high-intensity workout and pushing it again, and doing this repeatedly. Though I highly recommend a high-intensity workout within one's capacity, I constantly warn people against overtraining without adequate rest between workout sessions. I regularly come across many men and women in their forties and fifties who overtrained when they were in their twenties and thirties and are now facing severe irreparable knee, back, shoulder, and other problems.

Avoid exercises which waste your time and do not challenge you

Recently, I was in a Mumbai park which has a nice jogging track. I was waiting for my students to show up as it was our running day. I sat there, observing pot-bellied men and overweight women walking about leisurely and doing gentle exercises and gentle yoga postures.

While it is great to be walking or doing easy stretches in the fresh air and it is essential to include gentle yoga postures in your routine as they have numerous benefits, it does not do much for your overall fitness or for getting you back into shape. It is important to push yourself—raise your heart rate, push the muscles beyond their present capacity, if you wish to improve your fitness or get into better shape.

Even if you are just walking, after walking at an easy pace for sometime increase the pace and let your heart rate go up a bit. Walk up an incline once in a while to push yourself further.

Even if you wish to just practise yoga postures, after doing the asanas that are easy for you, attempt some asanas that are difficult and try to perfect them.

If you have ample time to devote to exercise then do a gentle walk followed by yoga postures on alternate days and do an elaborate workout—including cardiovascular endurance, strength, and flexibility—on other days.

If you have limited time to invest in a workout then be very careful with your choice of exercise. Make sure the exercise is addressing your needs according to your strengths and weaknesses. If you have very short time to devote, then make it a high-intensity workout and find a way to include all elements— strength, stamina, and flexibility. And work particularly on your body's weak points. If, for example, you have stiff muscles, then don't just keep doing strength exercises which is already your forte. Pay extra attention to the flexibility exercises for the larger part of your workout.

I have observed that though most men have naturally stronger but stiffer bodies, they prefer to work more on strength exercises and shy away from flexibility exercises, as they are embarrassingly difficult and awkward for them. Women, on the other hand, are naturally more flexible but are generally not so good on the strength front. I see many women with excellent flexibility still focusing only on stretching exercises instead of working on strength training.

I often see young people who are slightly overweight avoiding jogging and preferring to do a brisk walk instead. The most common reason for this is that they feel awkward as their body, in its present shape and fitness level, is really struggling while running. On the other hand, brisk walking comes quite easily.

The surest way to improve your fitness and get into better shape than you are right now is to do things that your body finds difficult and awkward in its present state. Move out of your comfort zone. Do things that are not easy for you.

If you are pressed for time to devote to workouts, and your goal is to improve your fitness and get into better shape then this is all the more reason to stay away from easy exercises, which are well within your comfort zone. They might just be wasting your time.

Avoid an all-or-nothing approach to exercise

Over the past ten years I have trained hundreds of people. A lot of them have attended my group sessions and workshops for different periods of time. There are a few things like running, Suryanamaskar, wake-up stretches, important yoga postures, basic kicks and punches, and certain freehand exercises that I try to make everyone master. I guide each person to identify their strengths and weaknesses and focus their attention on a few things that they should keep up on their own. I give them my customized handouts with photographed postures and a detailed workout plan tailored for them, a routine of the postures that would be beneficial to them, and the very minimum that they should keep up with even when they are travelling. My aim is to help everyone who comes to me get inspired to work out, understand their body—its strengths and weaknesses—and to give each person a customized plan to follow so that they can make a holistic workout routine a part of their life and continue to evolve it over time.

It feels great when I meet people I had trained years back and see that they are keeping fit by continuing to follow at least a part of the workouts.

Payal and Anusha, both talented designers, were not so fit and slim when they started to train with me in a group many years back. When I discontinued that group, I got them to note down the workouts they should continue on their own. I bumped into them after a gap of four years and was glad to see them fit and in great shape. They had been continuing their freehand workouts on their own, specially the running which I had introduced them to, several years back.

On the other hand, it is disheartening when I meet people I had worked out with who had become really fit at the time but have now stopped exercising altogether and are out of shape and unfit. A lot of their energy and my effort had gone into them achieving a good level of fitness and getting them into shape, all of which largely went to waste.

A lot of these people keep telling themselves that they will make time and start working out properly again very soon. While they keep planning for that day to come, they forget to do anything in the meantime. Come what may, they should at least keep up a minimum level of exercise so that they never slide back too much. In the Chapters that follow, I have elaborated on the kinds of exercises that can be accommodated even in a very busy schedule.

No matter how sincere you are about your workouts, you are bound to go off-track and miss a few sessions here and there due to unavoidable reasons. The key is to keep coming back and starting again. Don't keep looking for ideal conditions to start. Don't wait for the rains to stop first, just run up and down the stairs. Do just 20 minutes of yoga postures or a cardio or strength workout, whatever you feel like, right at home, or wherever you are. Don't let anything come in the way and stop you from doing at least *something*. It needn't always be an elaborate one-hour workout. Don't wait for years to take out half an hour everyday for breathing exercises, just do three minutes every day rather than not doing it at all.

Facts and Myths

When I start to train someone new or meet people socially who need advice on fitness, I am usually asked a few common questions. I think it's vital to clarify some of these common fitness misconceptions.

Q) Are running and taking the stairs bad for the knees?
Running and climbing are natural movements which are great for your muscles and heart. If you are fit and you're running and taking the stairs correctly, these movements are not harmful. However, if you are thumping your feet hard on the ground then it is surely bad for the joints in the long run. Make sure you're light on your feet. If you can hear your footsteps noticeably, you're running incorrectly.

Too much of running and stair climbing can be bad for the knees of certain people who are extremely overweight, who have weak knees, or who are doing the movement with wrong technique. Someone who's in their fifties or even forties and has never run before needs to very gradually introduce that movement to their joints and muscles; otherwise they'll be prone to injury. A person can continue running into their seventies and eighties, which many marathon runners the world over do. An 86-year-old man ran the full Mumbai marathon (42 km) successfully. Incidentally, he started running only in his sixties!

Q) Is walking or jogging on concrete bad for the knees?

If someone's running technique is wrong they will perhaps damage their joints sooner on a hard surface than they will on a soft mud track. But they will damage their knees on the soft track too. So injury has less to do with the track surface than running technique.

When we hear the thud of our feet while running, our joints are being jarred with each movement. When we run with the right technique, it is the muscles that do the work and act as shock absorbers causing minimal impact on the joints. Think about it. Marathon runners, including the ones who run into their seventies and eighties, run on concrete roads their whole lives, but nothing happens to their joints.

Another essential factor in being a good runner is to give sufficient rest to the muscles between runs. Running well also has a lot to do with stretching the key muscles so that they retain their elasticity. Running excessively makes the calves and hamstring muscles tighten and they need to be stretched adequately to prevent knee pain and injury.

Fauja Singh recently became arguably the oldest man to run a 42-km marathon at 100 years of age. Running on concrete roads for many decades has surely not damaged his knees!

Q) Will doing excessive crunches or working out on abs machines help me flatten my stomach?

Doing excessive crunches will only make your stomach muscles very strong which is not of much use, performance-wise, if your back and other muscles are not exercised accordingly. If you have a pot belly, it will remain well in its place no matter how many crunches you do. All it will do is create strong abdomen muscles beneath the flab.

Instead, you should be doing cardio exercises like running, cycling, brisk walking, skipping, and stair climbing to burn extra calories in order to flatten the stomach and lose weight in proportion to the rest of your body.

The other drawback in just doing excessive abdominal contractions is that it makes the stomach muscles much stronger as compared to the back muscles. This imblanace gives rise to lower back problems.

Q) Exercise makes us fit. If I overtrain and workout every day or twice a day, will it make me super fit?
Overtraining is as bad as undertraining, perhaps worse. Apart from triggering a burnout, over-exercising makes you perilously prone to injuries. To achieve the best fitness results, there is an optimum amount of exercise you must do. Anything beyond that gives diminishing returns and will make you weak, drain your energy levels, and cause injuries.

I see a lot of people addicted to working out, pushing their body day after day.

Apart from exercise and nutrition, the body needs sufficient rest to recuperate from vigorous exercise. Not giving your body enough rest between intensive workouts will cause unnecessary wear and tear of your joints. You may not feel the strain at present, but I've come across many people who've over exercised in their thirties and are now sitting it out with serious knee injuries in their forties and fifties.

Q) Just look at his six-pack! Isn't he incredibly fit?

Having a chiselled six-pack and being very muscular are not the only criteria of being fit, or for that matter, even very strong. This is the case particularly if those popping muscles have been developed the way a professional bodybuilder trains—by isolating muscle groups and not necessarily paying much attention to stretching and cardiovascular endurance exercises. As I mentioned in the earlier chapter, a professional bodybuilder's body is meant, mostly, for show. That is the main purpose of their training. On the other hand, an athlete or a sportsperson's training is for performance. So apart from strength, the athlete's fitness routine involves a good amount of exercises for flexibility, speed, and stamina. A person may be muscular but if they do not have good flexibility or stamina, they can't really be considered completely fit.

Many actors and models have proven that visible six-pack abs and overly well-defined muscles are achievable by putting in hard work. Our leading sportspeople put in much more hard work and time into their fitness workouts and training. Just think about it—why don't all our leading sportspeople or even elite soldiers, for that matter, sport visible six-pack abs if it would in any way enhance their physical performance?

Q) But she's so thin. She must be really fit! Isn't it the same thing?

Again, being thin and being fit are two very different things. I've come across many people who are thin but terribly unfit compared to someone who might not be so thin. Fitness is not about being thin or muscular, but about strength, flexibility, stamina, speed, fast reflexes, and balance. Only a person who has a good balance of all these factors, and can apply it functionally, can be called fit. Athletes, gymnasts, and most sportspeople epitomize fitness.

Q) Aren't fruits, coconut water, dry fruits, potato, banana, and other such natural foods also fattening as they have sugar, carbohydrates and are high in calories? Should I avoid them?

Understand one basic thing. Let's say a natural food in its raw form contains the same amount of calories as say a biscuit, a slice of bread, or some other processed food to start with. Our body needs to do some work burning some calories to break down natural foods, including bananas and potatoes, in order for these foods to release energy in the body. Fruits and other natural raw foods release energy slowly in the body as our body breaks them down. Highly refined foods such as white sugar do not need to be broken down by the body, which results in direct and sudden increase in blood sugar which is very harmful to the body. Moreover, natural foods have more nutrients and fibre which aids a healthier functioning of the body.

Whenever you have a choice, it is always healthier to opt for natural and least-processed food. Highly processed food is unnatural and creates havoc with the internal functioning of the body, making you overweight and prone to many diseases such as diabetes.

Q) Isn't exposure to sunlight harmful?

I can't emphasize the importance of sunlight enough. It is the greatest source of energy—a 'life force' for all life on our planet. Yes, excess of everything can be harmful, including exposure to sunlight, but some of it is very essential to our health, well-being, and radiance. Among several other benefits, it is the best source of Vitamin D, which helps us absorb calcium from food, which in turn strengthens our bones.

The air we breathe these days has harmful pollutants in it along with the oxygen. Just as we do not stop breathing that air, we should not shy away from the sun.

Many health problems being faced by people, especially in big cities like Mumbai are due to not getting enough direct sunlight.

Q) I am trying to lose weight. Should I totally avoid carbohydrates and fat, and just have a protein diet?

For a very brief period perhaps you could possibly try something like that. But if you sustain a diet which is totally deficient in one or more of the essential components of a balanced healthy diet—proteins, carbohydrates, vitamins, minerals, and fat—it will be harmful to your body in the long run. Your weight loss with such diets will be accompanied by harm to your internal system and organs. Moreover, the weight loss with such drastic and unhealthy measures will be temporary, and will come back with a vengeance within a few months or years.

A healthy and long-term weight loss is achieved by cutting down excess calories, especially in the form of white sugar and other processed as well as fried foods.

Q) I have cut down on white sugar in my tea and stopped eating fried stuff. Can I continue to have diet colas, brown bread, high-fibre biscuits and other food stuff with 'low sugar', 'low fat', 'low calorie', or 'enriched with minerals' written on them?

The biggest blunder that people make while cutting down on calories is that they blindly trust any food packet that says 'diet', 'low sugar', 'low fat', 'high fibre', 'enriched with minerals', and so on. A lot of these are mostly commercially driven products which trick the consumer. Something that is low in sugar might be full of processed carbohydrates which will readily convert to sugar once consumed. The 'high fibre' or 'low fat' food might actually be high in sugar. So minimize your intake of all processed food. Be very careful of even the small amount you might eat. Even the 'brown' bread that we get in the market is usually not as healthy as it claims.

Q) Is running on the treadmill the same as running outside? I want to train for the half marathon. Is it ok if I practise for it on the treadmill?

Running on the treadmill is not the same as running out in the open. It is not a good idea to predominantly run on the machine in preparation for running outdoors, particularly in a marathon. I have seen so many people who regularly run long distances on the treadmill struggling to run a fraction of that on real ground outside. Many of them are shocked and frustrated, as they are under the misconception that running on the treadmill is an absolute substitute to running outdoors.

A treadmill runs on electricity. The belt or the surface underneath your feet keeps moving towards you, unlike real ground outside. Just like a suitcase comes towards you on an airport baggage conveyor belt without any effort of its own, with every step you take on the treadmill, the forward leg comes back without any effort. You just have to lift the back foot forward again, which will again be brought back by the machine. The electrical power puts in the effort that you would otherwise have to if you were running outdoors.

When you walk or run on the road outside, the leg that's forward has to work harder. The muscles are being used in a specific way to propel the back leg forward each time. On a treadmill, the muscles of the legs are used in a totally different way as the surface below your feet is pulling your forward leg back each time. So although it'll feel like you're running as much as you might on solid ground, using electrical power makes walking or running on the treadmill comparatively very easy and in fact wholly different in the way your muscles are being used.

Running on the treadmill is not a natural movement and overdoing it is not great for you in the long run. Unless it is raining or snowing outside, just head out to the park nearby or even the road outside your house for your brisk walk or run.

Q) What is the right running technique? What are the right running shoes? What is this concept of barefoot running?
Before the modern highly cushioned running shoe was invented, human beings were largely running barefoot or with very minimal footwear. When you run barefoot, you will discover your natural running movement in which you will be landing on the mid foot and front part of your foot rather than your heel. This is the right technique of running. The running shoes with highly padded soles and heels that we get today enable us to run in a way that causes our heels to hit the ground first. This is wrong and a cause of many running-related injuries. You should buy shoes which enable

you to easily run with the right technique of landing on the mid and front of your feet, rather than the ones which have such thick heels that force you to land on the heel.

Barefoot running is gaining popularity as it reduces the chances of injuries caused by the over-cushioned running shoes which cause us to run with a wrong technique, unless we are very conscious of applying the right technique when running. When running barefoot, we are instinctively forced to run with the right technique as it would be painful to land on the heel.

Since we are so used to running with shoes, it is tough and perhaps not practical to suddenly start running barefoot. However, it is a great idea to run barefoot whenever you get a chance. When you are on the beach, grass, or nice mud surface—take off your shoes and run! It is sheer joy and very rejuvenating to do that and you will discover the right running technique which you should replicate even when you have your shoes back on.

An important argument in favour of barefoot running is that while running barefoot, you are able to feel the surface you are running on and the body adjusts the running technique accordingly. When running barefoot on a hard surface, you will be forced to be light on your feet, thereby reducing the chances of injury to your ankle, knee, and hip joints. I have seen many people with fancy running shoes run past me with a thumping sound—landing so hard that they are jarring their joints, causing progressive damage to them over the years. They wouldn't be able to land so hard running barefoot even if they wanted to as it would hurt immediately! When you are running barefoot, the soles of your feet sense the ground, send a signal to your brain, which in turn sends a signal to your body to be light on its feet to avoid damaging your joints.

You won't find extensive studies comparing the results of shoes versus barefoot running but a little experiment running with and without shoes will confirm what I am saying here is simple common sense. I strongly recommend walking and running barefoot on grass and sand whenever you get a chance as it is very healing for the body. The soles of our feet have extensive nerve endings which get soothed and stimulated, resulting in rejuvenation of the whole body, when in contact with natural surfaces like grass and sand.

Weight Loss Simplified

The amount of information, in all possible permutations and combinations, floating around on the much-talked-about issue of weight loss can be scary and bewildering for anyone. A lot of people are trying to sell easy, effortless, and magically fast ways to lose weight.

The truth is, to lose the weight you have acquired over a period of time will take time. And effort. That is, if you want to lose it in a healthy way. The shortcuts—magic diets, pills, and machines—will only harm your health in the long run. Shortcut weight-loss methods are temporary and the weight will inevitably come back, with a vengeance, if not in a few months then in a few years.

Losing weight isn't easy or fast. But it can be made easy, or easier, once you have a basic understanding of what it entails.

I've simplified weight loss into just four prominent principles. Follow these. They are your only elixir.

Burn: More Than You Eat

Several fads have come and gone and several more will come, become passé and redundant. This diet, that diet, avoid carbs, just eat proteins, juice diets, and so on. In this ever-changing scenario of what works and what doesn't, there is one thing that will always hold true.

To lose weight, burn more calories each day than what you are consuming.

This also means that you must drastically cut down on high-calorie food: everything containing processed white sugar, refined oil, processed butter, white rice, and processed wheat–maida, should be avoided. This would include biscuits, cakes, most breads, and many other ready-to-eat packaged foods.

By and large, everything natural and non-processed can be eaten more liberally than anything that is processed.

Natural foods, even if high in calories, have far more nutrients. Very importantly, the body burns more calories in the process of breaking down natural foods like nuts, salads, fruits, and whole grains. On the other hand, white sugar and other processed foods add empty calories to the body.

Exercise: To Raise Your Metabolic Rate

For the fastest, healthiest, and long-term weight loss results, you should be exercising to burn more calories.

Though all exercise is good, you need to focus more on cardiovascular exercises—exercises that raise your heart rate and get you out of breath. When you do a sustained cardio activity like brisk walking or jogging, and keep your heart rate high for 20 to 30 minutes, apart from burning a lot of calories, your metabolic rate also goes up. The metabolic rate refers to the rate at which you burn calories. Significantly, your metabolic rate remains high for almost twenty-four hours after you have finished high-intensity cardio exercise. Even short bursts of high-intensity cardio activity like climbing a few flights of steps quickly raises the metabolic rate. An inactive lifestyle devoid of consistent cardio activity makes the metabolism sluggish. If we consume processed high-calorie food in addition to leading a sedentary lifestyle, the kilos start piling up fast.

Additional exercises for strength and flexibility are great but when you want to lose weight, cardiovascular exercise is the most important. But remember, any exercise which doesn't get your heart rate up, like just picking up dumb-bells or only doing crunches with the hope of attaining a flat stomach won't help. Similarly going for a leisurely walk, which does not get your heart rate up won't help much. Walk the way people walk at Mumbai train stations, speeding up to catch their train. If you are not used to walking or running at all, you can start gradually for a few days till the muscles and joints get used to that movement. Just don't walk *too* slowly, or you might miss the train of getting into shape!

Breathe: To Harmonize Your Hormones

It's not always true that a person who is overweight eats more or is more inactive than a person who is thin. There are many other factors at play. One factor is the metabolic rate, which I've touched upon earlier. Then there are the reasons of hereditary, genetic factors, and certain diseases. Another important factor is the possibility of an internal chemical imbalance in the body. It is possible that the secretion of different glands in the body might be out of sync due to, among other factors, stress. This might very well be causing undue weight gain. The malfunctioning of the thyroid gland has become a major factor which contributes to weight gain. Often, this is in spite of someone being meticulous with exercise and diet.

To counter this and regulate the secretion of different glands in the body, it is important to practise specific breathing exercises, meditation, and relaxation techniques to balance the nervous system and other internal functions of the body which might be out of order.

Traditional yoga techniques, aimed at creating a balance at every level in the body, are very effective in addressing this imbalance. In particular, Pranayama (breathing techniques); static and twisting postures, which activate digestive organs and glands; Shavasana and other asanas specifically for relaxation; and slow rhythmic movements, which involve breathing and movement coordination, are all excellent. A practice like tai chi can also prove to be very beneficial.

Breathing and other relaxation techniques also reduce anxiety, which prevent you from overeating, from eating when not needed, and reduce craving for sugar and junk food, which inevitably leads to weight gain. I highly recommend practising the Anulom-Vilom pranayam on a regular basis after learning it from a good teacher.

Make sure that you are in a relaxed state of mind before eating a meal. A few deep breaths before you start to eat will help your mind relax.

Detoxify: To Feel And Be Light

When you are overweight, you would be inclined towards inactivity. Inactivity prevents the body from getting rid of toxins.

An accumulation of toxins in the body leads to many diseases. It's a vicious cycle.

While attempting to lose weight, it's a good idea to follow a detoxification processes. Flushing out the toxins accelerates the process of getting into shape.

While exercise and becoming active itself starts a detoxification process, you should complement it with other practices which aid detoxification of the body and uncluttering the mind. It's the same thing as deciding to get your home repaired and painted—it's a natural instinct to clean it thoroughly as well.

Make positive lifestyle changes like waking early, getting adequate sleep, overcoming unhealthy habits like smoking, and incorporating healthy ones that I have mentioned in the first Chapter. Get in touch with nature and allow the body to regain its natural biological rhythm.

Drink lots of water and fluids, eat seasonal fruit, get enough sleep, eat frequent light meals, go for a massage or just walk barefoot on grass or sand. Include lemon, honey, aloe vera, and amla into your diet. These aid detoxification.

A word of caution.

Firstly, do not overdo anything. If you suddenly start eating lots of fruits, salads, and sprouts you might just harm your body. The body will not react well to abrupt changes. So introduce the changes gradually. Let the body ease into it and be aware of how it is reacting to each change. Some things which might be good for someone else might not suit you. Remember, we are all made differently.

Secondly, know that for most of us who've ignored our health for a long time, the body and internal organs are in a state of abuse. They are filled with toxins. The body might start resisting at first or start reacting by making you want to sleep more. You might even get a fever, a boil, a runny nose, start sweating excessively, even throw up, or get an upset stomach. Brave this, get adequate rest, and then gently get back to it. Do get medical help for something severe, but any apparent side effects will mostly be a reaction of the body and a process of throwing out toxins.

Do bear in mind that when you plan a sudden detoxification through diet, exercise, yoga, and other therapeutic processes, keep aside some time to recuperate and heal from the process.

Ahmed, my barber, who I meet about once a month, has been struggling to reduce his slightly protruding belly. A pot belly is a very common problem amongst men. From time to time, Ahmed asks me for advice on how to reduce his stomach. When he first brought up the subject, I just told him to cut down on fried and sugary foods. Stop eating those oily snacks like samosas from outside, I told him. He followed my advice by starting to carry home-cooked food, avoided those multiple cups of chai with sugar and the oily snacks from outside and sure enough, his belly started shrinking a bit. The next month, he asked me if he could do something more. I told him that instead of taking public transport every day, he should start brisk walking to and from home to his place of work. He followed this, which not only helped him shed more weight but significantly boosted his energy levels. The motivated person that he is, the last time I met him he asked me if there was still something he was doing wrong. What more can I improve? I probed a bit further into his daily routine. I told him to eat a heavier breakfast and light dinner, something he was not doing at the moment. Then I figured out the biggest mistake he was making. Apart from the brisk walk in the morning and evening, he was totally inactive through the rest of the day—just standing while giving a haircut and sitting around the rest of the time. Start moving around more, through the day, I told him. Just walk around the shop in your breaks to keep up your metabolic rate. This made a lot of sense to him and he incorporated my advice with immediate effect!

As you work towards getting slimmer and fitter, I'd encourage you, like Ahmed, to introduce healthy changes gradually into your life, instead of all in a day!

Spine, Breath, and True Fitness

Spine

Your backbone is the backbone of your fitness. The state of your spine is one of the most important indications of your state of well-being.

Think about it. It's the basic, most essential framework of your body. It protects and directly affects the nervous system, which, in turn, affects the functions of all the organs in the body. If the spine is not in good condition—strong, supple, and well aligned—one cannot experience true well-being.

The spine is the main channel of energy flow of the prana—the 'life force'—which the Chinese call 'chi' and the Japanese 'ki'. The chakras—or main energy centres—of this 'pranic' energy in the body are along the spine, which in turn determine the aura of a person. A harmonious flow of energy along the chakras gives a person a very distinct glow.

Just because the spine is hidden at the back of the body and is not visible—it gets sorely neglected. We first notice the excess fat on the stomach. We try desperately to reduce it, and in our attempt to get ripped abs, we do loads of crunches. We work on strengthening and toning, exercising our arms, shoulders, legs, and other muscles visible to us. In the process, we go on ignoring and sometimes even worsening the state of our back.

I am not surprised by the popularity of the physical aspect of yoga, as working on the spine is an integral part of the practice. After a yoga session, many people start feeling lighter, more energetic, and good about themselves. This is mainly because they stretch, arch, twist, and strengthen their spine, which sadly is a much-ignored part of most exercise routines. In most workouts, too much emphasis is given on strength training and not enough on flexibility exercises. This ultimately results in a stiff and choked up spine which, in turn, leads to reduced energy levels and feeling less fit, no matter how toned and fit you might look externally.

When I start to train someone I gauge the state of their spine in the very first session. I make sure to include specific exercises to get their spine in good condition when I devise their overall fitness routine. I see too many people in their twenties

and thirties living with the spines of 70-year-olds. It's tragic to see such young people, many of who are thin or very muscular, living with spines that are in pitiable condition. This affects their well-being on every level, and the worst of it is that they don't even realize that they are living a life as stifled as the condition of their spine.

The age of your spine is your real age. If you start working on your spine and get it into good shape, you will feel young, no matter what age you are!

Breath

Another silent, subtle, and humble function in our body is too often ignored in many exercise routines—breathing.

How we breathe is fundamental to our well-being and fitness. It is extremely important to know whether you are breathing well and deeply enough. Once you take charge to improve your health and fitness, it'll be absolutely essential that you include exercises which improve the way you breathe.

If your breathing is shallow, you are leading a compromised and suffocated existence. Most of us as adults start taking shallow breaths, reducing our oxygen intake, which results in reduced energy levels.

Moreover, our breathing is directly related to our state of the mind. Fast and shallow breath results in an anxious state of mind. Relaxing and centring the mind is very difficult, but if we practise breathing techniques and endeavour to make our breathing deep, it leads to better energy distribution, a relaxed state of mind and regulates secretions of different glands in the body. Even if you generally breathe well, you should practise deep breathing on a regular basis. This way, you'll be working towards making your subconscious breathing pattern deeper. Your health will improve as a result of a more relaxed state of mind and nervous system.

Just as I look at the condition of the spine when I begin training someone, I also observe their present state of breathing. If I find that the person's breathing is shallow or too fast, I make sure to add extra exercises in their workout routine to enhance their breathing and lung capacity.

Once you have reasonably improved your breathing, you can use deep breathing, breath awareness, and breath control as tools to take your wellness, peace of mind, and efficiency to another level. It will help you stay calm, joyful, and relaxed. You'll learn how to improve your performance and productivity, while also learning how to not only conserve energy, but increase it. And, of course, because you'll be less stressed out, you're bound to have that extra glow.

True Fitness

In this era of profit-driven health, beauty, fitness 'knowledge', and products, it's crucial that we develop and use our intuition. We need to be aware enough to choose what is actually good for us over that which is being sold to us as true fitness.

Looking at the physiques of film stars, models, superheroes, and commercially motivated ads for fitness products has largely distorted our idea of fitness today.

The harmful effects of cigarettes and alcohol are widely known and do not worry me as much as the machines and foods, which are detrimental to our bodies and are being sold as health and fitness products. It is the general notion that women who are thin and men who are muscular are fit. And it's easy to understand why. We live in a world where the visual medium dominates and if you have to *show* fitness, it's easy to show a skinny girl or muscular man.

Being a martial artist, I've been a great admirer of the legendary martial artist and actor—Bruce Lee. Although he was super fit and already a great martial artist, when Bruce Lee was to star in a film as the action hero, his producer told him that he was too lean and skinny and would have to put on more muscle to make his power believable to the audience.

The truth is, like I have explained earlier, being extraordinarily muscular or thin is no measure of a person's fitness. True physical fitness is a combination of several factors—strength, flexibility, stamina (by which I mean cardiovascular endurance)—and also includes elements such as balance, reflex, and speed.

Holistic fitness is further inclusive of overall health, well-being, and a harmonious flow of energy in the body. Watch the body language of a sportsperson, athlete, dancer, or gymnast. They're lean, yet muscular. Their movements have a certain grace. They naturally exude true fitness.

If someone is to be called truly fit, they should be above average in all these aspects. Some people might score much higher in one aspect than another. A long-distance runner might have more stamina than a long jumper. A wrestler might have more overall strength than a marathon runner. A ballet dancer might score more on balance, coordination, and flexibility. But one thing that would be common and true for them all is that they would be at least above average in the broad aspects of strength, flexibility, and stamina, qualifying them as 'fit'.

The emphasis in my workouts is on *overall fitness*, and I draw elements from athletic fitness training, martial arts, and the physical aspect of yoga. Sometimes the thinnest or the most overly muscular people to join my classes have been the most unfit to begin with as they lacked *overall fitness*.

A very fit-looking model, Shruti joined my group class. She had been working out in the gym—mostly weight training and running on the treadmill—regularly for many years. When she expressed the desire to join my class, I asked her, like I ask everyone, 'Have you been working out for your fitness previously?' She was half amused and half offended. 'Can't you make out?' came her reply. She was thin and had the ideal body that is frequently advertised as fit. When she began my classes, I realized that she indeed had average strength and above-average flexibility, but when I made my group run rounds of Mumbai's Jogger's Park, she could not run more than two rounds, whereas all the others in the group—not all as thin as her—could run ten rounds with relative ease. Of course, now, after a few months of athletic, all-round fitness training, her stamina is much better and she tells me that she's never felt fitter.

Then there have been instances where I have worked out with very muscular people who have been mainly into bodybuilding. Many of these people have been extremely poor in terms of flexibility and stamina and I have seen them struggle while trying to run, play a sport, or do even simple yoga postures. Though outwardly very muscular, they can't be called fit since flexibility and cardiovascular fitness is integral to fitness.

Being muscular isn't necessarily bad. However, we do need to make a distinction between stiff and supple muscles. Athletes, like short-distance sprinters, are usually also very muscular. The difference is that they have supple muscles which retain their elasticity.

This elasticity is achieved through a perfect balance of both strength exercises (contraction of muscles) and flexibility exercises (stretching the muscles). Since athletes include both types of exercises in their training, their muscles become hard when required and relax when not in use.

When devising our workouts we should work towards developing muscles like that of an athlete—supple muscles that are practically useful and make you both look good and feel good at the same time.

Real fitness to me is functional fitness. It is the ability to perform and do things using the body.

True fitness allows you to perform your day-to-day physical activities better. It prepares you for any strenuous activity—trekking, running up ten flights of steps, walking or running a few kilometres, lifting a heavy object, jumping over a wall, climbing up using a rope, pushing your car, or playing a sport. The list is endless.

Such fitness is achievable with the right combination of exercise, diet, and rest. During the unfortunate attacks in Mumbai on 26/11, we all saw our NSG commandos descending on to the targetted sites by sliding down a rope from their helicopters. Those commandos embody true fitness.

A few years ago I got an opportunity to run a five kilometer race with army jawans, which was a part of their regular training and was amazed at their level of fitness. And most of them had acquired absolutely lean physiques by playing various sports and freehand outdoor exercises, including running and push-ups, and not by working out with machines in the gym!

Instead of just aspiring to lose weight or targetting to acquire six-pack abs, I strongly propose you to aim for all-round functional fitness. It will certainly make you feel and look truly fit as well as attractive. That feeling will reflect on your face—a feeling that says you're truly fit, relaxed, and consequently, happy.

A Few Terms Explained

There are a few terms that I have used throughout the book. Here, I am listing those terms along with brief explanations.

Cardio: Cardio is the short form for cardiovascular exercise. Cardio exercises raise your heart rate and get you out of breath. Jogging, cycling, and stair climbing are examples of cardio exercise.

Warm-up: The warm-up has two parts. First, you heat up your body by doing a light cardio exercise like brisk walking or jogging. The second part of the warm-up incorporates some stretches and joint rotations to prepare the body for any strenuous activity such as a workout or a game of squash.

Contractions: A muscle can be stretched or contracted. While stretching a muscle improves flexibility and the range of motion of that particular muscle, contracting it improves its strength. Exercises such as push-ups, squats, crunches, etc, which strengthen particular muscles by contracting them are often referred to as 'contraction exercises' or simply 'contractions'.

Endurance or Stamina: Cardiovascular endurance, also known as aerobic fitness or stamina, is the ability to exercise continuously for extended periods without tiring. For example, if two people with different stamina levels are climbing ten flights of steps at a reasonably fast pace, the one with low endurance or stamina will get out of breath midway and will need to stop to catch a breath, whereas the person with good endurance will be able to go on without getting out of breath or getting tired.

Dynamic posture: Dynamic postures are yoga postures which are done slowly and with awareness, involving the coordination of your breath along with the movement.

Static posture: Static postures are yoga postures in which the final position is held with stillness, grace, and normal deep breathing for a long duration of time, which could be anywhere from a few seconds to a minute to several minutes.

Jogging/Brisk walking: There are five common cardio exercises—walking at a normal pace, brisk walking, jogging, running, and sprinting. Jogging falls in the middle and is a wonderful exercise that can be done at any age.

Jogging is extremely beneficial for several reasons as it incorporates a hopping movement, which is a step up from the movement of brisk walking.

Don't try to go fast at the start. Jogging is not running fast. Consciously go slower than you might imagine.

If continuous jogging is too difficult for you right now, alternate between brisk walking and jogging. After walking for 3 minutes, try jogging for 1 minute, then go back to brisk walking. With practise, gradually increase the jogging duration. Whenever I use the term *jogging* in the workouts, you can substitute it with *brisk walking interspersed with jogging*.

If even jogging interspersed with walking is genuinely too difficult for you at present, then stick to brisk walking whenever I have mentioned jogging. Brisk walking is also extremely beneficial. But make sure it is brisk enough to raise your heart rate.

Freehand: Freehand exercises are any exercises that do not require a machine or elaborate equipment. Running outdoors is a freehand exercise. Yoga stretches are freehand.

This term is usually more commonly used for strength training. In freehand strength training you use your own body weight to strengthen muscles, like when you do push-ups and squats. The strength training exercises in the gym, which use machines, are not freehand exercises.

The exercises I have recommended throughout this book are freehand as I find freehand exercises to be the most natural, healthy, and time efficient. Moreover, their results are long lasting.

Wake-Up stretches: *Wake-up stretches* is a term I have coined for a series of morning stretches I've adapted to suit a modern lifestyle. Wake-up stretches activate the spine and are best done shortly after you wake up. Watch a cat or dog waking up from a sleep. They immediately do one or two stretches before they are ready to run around. Wake-up stretches are inspired by this and are one of the most important things that you can absorb from this book.

Suryanamaskar: Suryanamaskars are a series of ten yoga poses to be performed in a sequence. When

I say ten, I am not counting the starting namaskar position. These ten postures complete one cycle.

The Suryanamaskar is extremely beneficial—it activates all the muscles from head to toe, increases blood circulation, and most importantly—harmonizes the flow of pranic energy in the body.

Suryanamaskars are excellent for the spine and like I mentioned earlier, the state of your spine dictates your health and well-being.

They can be difficult for someone who is not very fit, is stiff, has weak muscles, or an injury, especially of the spine.

If practising Suryanamaskar seems very difficult in the beginning, I would advise you to practise other easier yoga postures before attempting the Suryanamaskar. When you do attempt it, make sure your body is slightly warmed up.

Pranic energy or prana: Whenever I refer to the fact that yoga postures, meditation, and deep breathing harmonize the pranic energy in the body, I'm referring to an invisible, subtle energy flow, a life force, which breathes life into our body. When it leaves the body, it becomes lifeless or dead. This energy is present in everyone who is alive, and through certain practices, can be expanded and harmonized.

When you see a person whose energy flows

in harmony, you notice they have a subtle glow emanating from within. This glow is often also called the aura of that person.

This is an ancient eastern concept. While in India this energy is called pranic energy, in China it is called *chi* whereas the Japanese refer to it as *ki*.

Functional fitness: Functional fitness is the kind of fitness that actually translates to you being able to do day-to-day activities more efficiently and gracefully. It also helps you to use your body efficiently in physically challenging situations like running, pushing your car, playing sports, defending yourself in a fight, or climbing few flights of stairs.

Soldiers and sportspeople embody functional fitness as their training is geared towards physical performance.

Traction exercises: These are exercises which gently pull the vertebrae of the spine apart. More enhanced traction exercises are used in physiotherapy for spinal injuries such as a slipped disc.

The traction exercises I have shown in the book are simple ones which prevent such injuries and keep your spine in good condition.

Core muscles: Core muscles are mainly muscles in the mid section of your body—stomach, back, hips, and particularly the lower back, which give the basic stability to your body. These muscles are not very visible but play a very important role in your functional fitness and posture.

Someone with bulging visible biceps, calves, quadriceps, and abs can have weak core muscles, making that person prone to injuries and poor in functional fitness.

Dari:

Many times in the book, I have said you can choose to use a dari instead of a yoga mat for exercises and yoga postures.

A dari is a thick mat made of cloth which is thick enough to comfortably put your knees on yet not so soft that your knees sink into it.

Major muscle groups (Diagram):

In the diagram, I have only shown the muscles which I have particularly referred to by their names while explaining exercises.

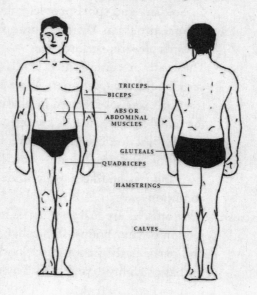

TRICEPS
BICEPS
ABS OR ABDOMINAL MUSCLES
GLUTEALS
QUADRICEPS
HAMSTRINGS
CALVES

Your Present State

Common Roadblocks

There are some common roadblocks that prevent many of us from even starting exercise. Let's begin by addressing some of them.

I have observed that recurring pain in the lower back and behind the neck is one of the biggest factors preventing people from starting a workout routine since any strenuous exercise can make that pain worse. Among other roadblocks, I have particularly explained dealing with recurring back pain in more detail.

Even if you have not experienced back pain, don't skip reading this section. It will be beneficial to you in evolving a potentially injury-free workout routine. Doing the exercises I have outlined will ensure your back continues to stay pain free and in optimum condition. Moreover, if you do feel the slightest back pain in the future you will be able to nip it in the bud.

Lower back and cervical (behind the neck) pain

Thanks to our modern lifestyle—which includes driving, watching TV, or working on the computer—we all suffer from some kind of cervical (neck) or lower back pain. If this pain is ignored, over a period of time it can cause a pretty serious and extremely painful condition requiring physiotherapy or, in some extreme cases, even surgery. If you have recurring cervical and lower back pain, then you need to be extra careful while starting to exercise. Though you have to be very careful, it is, ironically, only through exercise that you'll be able to cure yourself.

You need to address this issue before you start any high-intensity exercise, and be particularly aware of what *not* to do while exercising. Incorrect exercise could make your condition worse. The good news is that it is possible, in most cases, to correct the imbalance and gradually work towards an intense exercise routine.

Over time, bad posture or excessive forward bending of the neck or the lower spine can cause an imbalance. If we don't pay heed to the warning signals of the spine, which manifest themselves in the form of slight pain, and don't correct the imbalance, then the spine goes into a spasm. During a spasm the back muscles contract abnormally causing excruciating pain as the nerves in that area feel the extreme pressure of that contraction. This forces you to immobilize the spine and rest it. This is a saving mechanism of the body to force you to take action and restore a balance to prevent further and permanent damage.

If you suffer from severe neck or lower back pain, then give your back or neck proper care and attention, at least for a week, and take corrective measures before you start exercising. Make sure you avoid movements with a jerk, and be particularly careful during forward-bending movements. Always stop a movement in case you feel pain.

Many of us who have bad posture or sit for long hours at the computer bending forward ignoring back pains run the risk of inviting such back spasms. In this case, suddenly starting a high-intensity workout may trigger the spasm, which at the outset might seem to be due to the workout but it is in fact, a spasm which was a long time coming. It was only precipitated in the course of the workout. If not through a workout, your back would have given way trying to lift a suitcase, which is not the real cause but just the last straw in you neglecting your spine and not heeding its gentle warnings.

If you have a weak, stiff, or painful cervical or lower back then practise the following exercises for a few days in preparation for any strenuous exercise. Start strenuous workouts when the pain is gone.

Resting positions

When the lower or upper back is in pain, the following resting positions are very effective for relief.

Crocodile position 1 (Makarasana variation 1)

Technique: Lie down on your stomach with your hands under the chin.

Crocodile position 2 (Makarasana variation 2)

Technique: Lie down on your stomach. Rest on your elbows, your chin supported with your hands. This slightly arched position is very good for your spine.

The two crocodile positions are good both for lower back and cervical pain. However, if you feel any pain in the position, then avoid it for the time being.

Shavasana position

Technique: Lie down on your back with your palms facing upward and consciously make all your muscles lose. Be aware of your body and your breathing. Relax in that

position for a few minutes. If the lower back is in discomfort and pain then bend the knees slightly. Alternatively, put a pillow under your legs. Listen to your body, listen to your spine, it will tell you what is the most comfortable resting position it wants to be in. Resting in that position will help the body heal itself.

Knees bent (variation)

Pillow under the legs (variation)

Pavanmuktasana position

Technique: Lying on your back, bend both knees, and press them towards your stomach gently. This is particularly very good to ease lower back pain.

Relax with neck support

Technique: Sit comfortably and put the neck back against a support at a comfortable angle to rest the neck. Adjust the height to make sure it does not strain the neck but makes it feel nice and comfortable. This position is particularly good for cervical pain.

In all the above relaxation positions, hold the posture for a few minutes. While you rest in these positions you will be helping the body to speed up its healing process.

Backward-bending exercises

Once the pain is less, gently start practising these exercises to correct the imbalance in your spine and to heal it further.

Bhujangasana (Cobra posture) starting position

Mid position

Final position

Technique: Start with lying down on the stomach with hands near the chest, as shown in the picture. Now slightly raise your neck and upper body without jerking as shown in the picture. Thereafter, use your hands to raise your body further and increase the arch on the back. Hold the final position for a few seconds and slowly come back to the starting position. Breathe in when you raise the body and breathe out when you come back to the starting position.

This cobra position or Bhujangasana is one of the best exercises you can do for your lower back and neck. Do it slowly, hold for a few seconds to a minute in the final position, and repeat it, at least six times. When you are holding it longer, you don't need to hold your breath, just breathe normally. Doing it on a regular basis will heal your spine and keep it in good condition.

These are a few other simple backward-bending exercises which are very good for your spine.

Standing backward bend

Technique: Stand with legs a little more than shoulder-width apart. Put the hands on your hips and arch backward. Hold for 5 to 10 seconds and come back to the starting position. Repeat this two to three times. You can practise this few times in the day, especially if your work requires you to work on the computer, which involves bending forward for long durations; take a break and practise this to recreate balance and ease your spine.

On-knees backward bend

Technique: Sitting with your knees on the ground, place your hands on the hips and gently arch back, keeping your balance. Hold a comfortable stretch in that position for a few seconds before coming back to the starting position and then repeat it once again.

While the above two exercises are particularly good for the lower back, these two 'shoulder and neck back' stretches are particularly good for the cervical area of the back.

Seated shoulder-and-neck backward stretch

Technique: Sitting comfortably, pull the shoulders back and simultaneously tilt the neck back. Look at the ceiling. Hold that gentle stretch for a few seconds. Repeat this three times. Practise this few times a day, particularly after a long duration of forward bending, like working on the computer.

Standing shoulder-and-neck backward stretch

Technique: Stand with legs shoulder-width apart. Interlock the fingers of your hands behind you and push them slightly downwards. Now pull your shoulders back and tilt the neck back to feel a gentle stretch on your shoulders and neck. Repeat this two times and hold the final position for a few seconds each time. Do this three to four times a day to ease your upper back.

Traction exercises for the back

Apart from backward bending, gentle vertical stretching or traction exercises which gently pull the vertibrae in your spine are immensely beneficial. The final streched position should be held for a few seconds and the exercises repeated four to six times.

Sitting traction exercise 1

Hand position

Technique: Sit comfortably and interlock your fingers as shown in the first picture. Raise your hands upwards to reach the final position as shown in the second picture. Do the movement slowly. In the final position you should feel a gentle upward pull on the spine. Hold the final position for a few seconds before coming back to the starting position. Repeat this three times. You should practise this about three times a day.

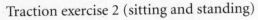

Traction exercise 2 (sitting and standing)

Hand position

Technique: Similar to the previous exercise, this time stretch the hands upwards while keeping your fingers interlocked with the palms facing up. Breathe normally and hold the stretch to the count of 10. Do this two to three times a day.

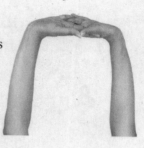

Lying down traction exercise

Technique: Lie down on your back with your hands stretched back above your head. Now stretch the hands

further upwards and at the same time push your heels downwards. Attempt to lengthen your body as much as possible, stretching both your hands and legs, and hold that position for a few seconds. Repeat this three times. After this, practise shavasana for a few seconds to relax.

Back-strengthening exercises

When the spine is free of pain and in better condition after few days of rest and subsequent backward-bending postures, the next step is to strengthen the back muscles to minimize the chance of spinal problems in the future.

The spinal strengthening and backward-bending postures should be practised on a regular basis to keep the spine in good condition

Back strengthening starting position

Back strengthening variation 1 (Ardha Vipreet Naukasana)

Back strengthening variation 2 (Poorna Vipreet Naukasana)

Technique (Variation 1): Start with lying down on your stomach with hands stretched in front of you. Raise the right hand and the left leg up as you breathe in to do the Ardha Vipreet Naukasana as shown in the picture. Come back to the starting position while breathing out. Now raise the left hand and the right leg similarly. Hold the final position for a second before coming down. You will feel the back muscles getting contracted in the final position. Repeat four to six times. Do not come up with a jerk, do it gently. Breathe in when you raise your hand and leg, breathe out when you come down. This is excellent for strengthening your back muscles.

Technique (Variation 2): If variation 1 is comfortable for you, then you can gradually try doing the Poorna Vipreet Naukasana. The procedure is similar. In this one, you raise both the legs and both the hands simultaneously while breathing in, hold it there and then come back to the starting position while breathing out.

You can do the variation 1, 3 to 6 times followed by variation 2, 4 to 6 times or according to your capacity. If the 'full boat posture' in too strenuous for you at present, then stick to variation 1 till your spine is strong and flexible enough to attempt it.

Practising strengthening exercises for your legs and arms will also indirectly help your spine heal and prevent it from getting injured in the future.

Doing day-to-day work, especially while picking up things from the floor, be aware to bend your knees and primarily use your leg muscles and arm muscles instead of letting the maximum strain come on your back.

You should practise squats on a regular basis to strengthen your leg muscles. These also help in strengthening the back further. Start easy according to your capacity. Do the movement very slowly and stop if you feel a pain in your back. Correct technique is very crucial. If unsure about your technique then consult an expert.

Squats

Starting position

Mid position

Final position

Technique: Keep your legs shoulder-width apart and parallel to each other. Start lowering your hips slowly as if you are moving in slow motion to sit on an imaginary chair.

In the final position, you are sitting on the imaginary chair with your knees at a ninety-degree angle. Hold your body in that position for a second and then slowly move back to the starting position. Start with 4 to 6 squats according to your capacity and gradually increase the repititions over a period of time.

Pooja, a student of mine, requested me to meet Akbar, a friend of hers who was facing a big dilemma.

Akbar is very passionate about horses. He owns a few horses and loves grooming and riding these amazing creatures. Due to excess weight, a largely sedentary lifestyle, and horse riding, his lower back packed up. He was advised surgery for his back and was told he might never be able to ride again. Akbar, who was an equestrian enthusiast, couldn't imagine a life without being able to ride horses.

I told him that for me to be able to help him, he would need to strictly follow my advice and be disciplined. We started with relaxation exercises like Shavasana and Pavanmuktasana to reduce the pain, then moved on to gentle backward-bending and traction exercises in a few days. Once his back was feeling better, we started back strengthening exercises as well as walking on the racecourse track amidst horses training for the races. Everyone at the racecourse seemed to know him, and due to his laid-back reputation, everyone was amused and pleasantly surprised to see him brisk walking early in the morning!

Within a month he was back to riding horses. As a thank you gesture, he very magnanimously offered me the use of his well-trained thoroughbred horses whenever I want. I have, of course, taken him up on the offer, and learnt riding on his well-groomed, beautiful, and extremely fit horses!

Shoulder, knee, ankle, and other injuries

If your injuries are not very recent and not very painful, and the doctor has not specifically stopped you from exercising, you must not let these come in the way of starting exercise. Begin at an easy pace and avoid putting excessive strain on your area of weakness. For example, if you have had a shoulder injury, then avoid excessive push-ups, but do walk. If your ankle or knee is weak or has had an injury, in the initial stages, be gentle when you're brisk walking. Concentrate more on lying-down exercises, which do not put a pressure on the knees or ankles. Add extra physiotherapy exercises, stretches, and slow rotations for the weak areas to recreate the balance. Make sure to warm up well before pushing yourself even slightly. Warming up greatly reduces the chances of further injury. You will find that your old injuries will get better and even cured with the correct exercise, especially with stretching and gentle yoga practice.

When you begin the 'One-Month Commitment' in the next chapter, avoid the exercises that put strain on the injured area. Avoid any movement that you think is aggravating your injury.

Listen to your body, listen to your doctor and physiotherapist, but do not make your injury an excuse to never begin an effective exercise routine.

I come across many people avoiding exercise just because they went to a doctor a long time ago with an injury and at the time, the doctor had told them to rest and avoid any strenuous activity.

Rakhi, a 22-year-old girl, started training with me. She said she wanted to get fit but had been advised by her doctor a while back to avoid running and climbing steps, so she was able to just do brisk walks and other gentle exercises, which would not strain the knee. She also wanted to lose weight and get into great shape. After a few sessions of gentle exercise, I made her start very light jogging, which did not cause her any discomfort and we slowly increased the intensity over a period of time. Now she is able to run effortlessly like someone her age ought to.

I must add here that a lot of patience is required to start exercising after an injury. You have to put strain on the affected area one step at a time. If you push it too much it will get worse. Therefore, traditional, gentle yoga works very well to help get back after an injury as it doesn't have jerky movements and works towards restoring balance without putting undue strain on the body.

I learnt an expensive lesson about aggravating injuries myself. In case of a sudden injury which makes you feel excruciating pain, it is foolish to brave it and keep exerting, and much wiser to listen to the body and rest the injured area to keep it from getting worse and to help the body start its healing process.

I had injured my knee very badly a few years ago while fighting in a state-level martial arts competition. I injured it during a fight but decided to continue fighting in the subsequent rounds as long as I was winning. In the process, my knee injury progressively worsened.

Though I won the tournament, I had greatly aggravated the knee injury and had to immobilize it for many days. Even after a month there was pain and the doctor advised more rest. When two months of rest too did not cure my pain, I travelled to meet my friend Augustine, who is a sports physiotherapist. An athlete himself, he *told me that I had rested my knee enough and it was time for me to attempt slow jogging and leg-strengthening exercises even if it was slightly painful. I did as he said and within a week my knee was fine. I was back to running and my normal exercise routine.*

Every injury is different and it's always prudent to seek a doctor's advice, but coming from a sports and martial arts background, I believe it is also important that we not make a big deal of an injury and let it stop us from anything in the long run. Having said that I also feel we should listen to our body, rest it when it's in pain, and understand that the body has its own healing mechanism. We should help the body heal itself and once we have rested an injury enough, we should gently get back to exercise. Resting beyond a point starts making the muscles weak, causing further problems.

Excessive weight

If you are excessively overweight, you need to start becoming strict with your diet and start exercising right away. You'll need to focus particularly on cardiovascular exercise which raises your heart rate—brisk walking, jogging, skipping, running up the stairs, or cycling. These exercises burn more calories and raise the metabolic rate, which is the healthiest way to lose weight.

Be careful and go easy when you start. Since there is a lot of pressure from the excess weight on your knees and ankles, you might injure yourself if you overstrain them suddenly.

Start at a gentle pace and intensity letting the joints and muscles get used to the movement. Rest your joints and muscles adequately. This will make them stronger over a period of time as you continue to intensify your workouts.

Before you start the 'One-Month Commitment' in the next chapter, you should start with eating a very low-calorie diet. Along with controlling your diet, go for a brisk walk for 30 to 45 minutes every alternate day for a week. This will prepare you for the 'One-Month Commitment'.

You might feel awkward and out of sync doing a lot of exercises due to excess weight but do not let that deter you. Do not avoid exercises like jogging outdoors just because you feel uncomfortable and ungraceful doing that at present. That very exercise will be the fastest way for you to get back into shape.

The beautiful Sonam Kapoor, whom I've had the opportunity to train for a few sessions while she was preparing for her debut film, had been overweight at one point of time but has worked hard and sweated it out to look the way she does today.

Other medical conditions

If you suffer from any other conditions such as very high or low blood pressure, heart problems, asthma, etc, then consult your doctor and follow the basic guidelines of what to avoid while exercising. Since this is a holistic workout with yoga at its core, it will be beneficial for any condition, but do follow basic precautions. Avoid or go easy while attempting certain exercises that might cause you harm or prevent you from moving towards better fitness. Listen to your body, it will give you a warning pain or discomfort if a particular movement has the potential to aggravate your condition. Do not do movements with a jerk and pay attention to the body so you are able to heed the instinctive warning signal in time. For example, if you have high blood pressure, you need to be aware enough to know when to stop pushing yourself further while working out. Avoid distractions like listening to loud music alongside working out so that you are able to listen to your body.

No matter what the injury or illness, don't make it an excuse to avoid all exercise. After you have rested enough, consult your doctor to find out the movements which should be avoided and start at least a gentle exercise routine and walking.

Find your strengths and weaknesses

A Workout to know Your Present State of Fitness

Before you begin the journey to get fit, it's important to know where you stand. The first thing I ask a person who is just starting to workout is whether they have any injuries or medical conditions. I then ask them if they are aware of their fitness strengths and weaknesses. Some are more aware than others and tell me they have a weak lower back, or tight hamstrings, or low stamina.

In the first session, I'll make them do a few yoga postures and freehand strength, flexibility, endurance, and balancing exercises. This way I get to gauge their strengths and weaknesses. Only then do I devise a customized routine accordingly. Most people who are unaware of their strengths and weaknesses discover it for themselves in the very first session.

For this session you will need to have a reasonably empty stomach. Wear lose, comfortable clothes. You'll need a yoga mat or a dari, and sports shoes. Keep around an hour for the following routine and don't rush through it. Try to do this around sunrise or sunset.

The Basic Warm-up

It is important to do a thorough warm-up, especially when you are beginning to exercise after a long gap. There are four stages to our basic warm-up to be done one after the other in the following sequence—Heating Up the Body 1, Warm-up Exercises 1, Heating Up the Body 2, and Warm-up Exercises 2.

Heating Up the Body 1

1. Wear your running or walking shoes and head out for a walk to a nearby park or just the road outside your house.
2. Walk at your normal pace for the first 7 minutes.
3. Then increase the pace for 3 minutes. At this point, your heart rate should go up.
4. Then, walk at a normal pace for 2 minutes again. Let your breathing rate normalize.

Warm-up Exercises 1

Standing toe touching (Dynamic Padahastasana)

Technique: Stand with your feet together. Raise your hands up and arch back while breathing in. Breathe out as you bend forward to touch your toes. If you feel a strain in your lower back or are unable to touch your toes, then bend the knees slightly as you reach for your toes.

Repeat three times

Bending knee—front and back—with support

Technique: Taking the support of a wall or something sturdy with your right hand, raise the left knee and bend it, pressing it with your left hand to get a good stretch. Put the left leg down and

now bend the knee, taking the left leg behind you using the left hand supported at the ankle to increase the stretch on your quardriceps. Hold this final position for a few seconds before you put your foot down. Repeat the same with your right leg.

Hold each stretch for 5 seconds on each leg

Ankle stretch

Technique: From a standing position, stretch one leg forward. Raise the toe upward and hold for 4 seconds. Now stretch the toe downwards and hold for 4 seconds.

Repeat two times with each leg

Ankle rotation

Technique: Starting in the same position as the ankle stretch, rotate the toe gently three times clockwise and three times anticlockwise. Repeat the same with the other leg.

Heating Up the Body 2

Now according to your capacity, either jog back home at a very light pace or walk back really fast. Walk fast like you are rushing to catch a train. When you get back home, try to climb a few flights of steps before proceeding to the next set of warm-up exercises.

This should take about 3 minutes

If you're finding it difficult to go out for a walk, you can alternatively do a bit of walking or spot jogging indoors, followed by climbing up and down the stairs for 'Heating Up the Body—1 and 2'. Don't tire yourself excessively, but you should sweat a bit and your heart rate should go up slightly.

Warm-up Exercises 2

Next, take off your shoes. Have a few sips of water at room temperature and spread out your dari or yoga mat. Open the window, but try not to switch on the fan. If you have to, then keep it on low. Do not switch on the AC.

Do the following warm-up stretches and rotations on your mat.

Side stretch

Technique: Stand with your feet little more than shoulder-width apart. Stretch to the side with one hand over your head and the other

79

hand sliding down along your leg on the other side.

Hold the stretch for 10 seconds on either side

Do the same stretch on the other side.

Side stretch with one hand back

Technique: This is similar to the earlier side stretch. Put the hand you were sliding down along your leg behind you as shown in the picture and repeat the side stretch on either side again.

Hold for 10 seconds on either side

Feet apart forward and backward bend

Technique: Keep your feet about double your shoulder-width apart. Push the hips

slightly back and stretch your hands forward as shown in the picture. Hold this stretch for 10 seconds. Now arch back with your hands on your hips. Hold the stretch for 10 seconds. Repeat this two times

Head-to-toe rotations

In the following stretches and rotations, we will activate and mobilize the joints and muscles from your head to toe, starting with the neck.

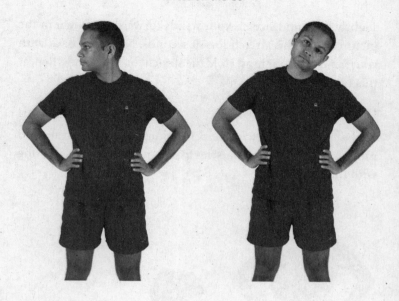

Neck stretches

Technique: Stand comfortably with your legs shoulder-width apart and put your hands on your hips. Gently stretch the neck upwards. Hold that position for 4 seconds, then move the neck down and hold it for 4 seconds. Repeat this twice.

Now turn the neck to either the left or the right, and hold there for 4 seconds. Then turn it to the other side and again hold for 4 seconds. Repeat twice.

Now tilt the neck to one side, hold for 2 seconds and then to the other side for 2 seconds. Repeat twice. Ensure that you don't jerk the neck while doing this. While holding each position, you should feel a gentle stretch in your neck muscles.

Shoulder rotation

Technique: Standing in the same comfortable position with feet roughly shoulder-width apart, raise the elbows upwards with fingers touching the

shoulders. In a slow, continuous movement, take the elbows up and back, making a full circle clockwise to come back to the starting position.

Repeat this clockwise shoulder rotation three times. Thereafter, do the rotation in the anticlockwise direction thrice. As with the neck rotations, don't do this movement with a jerk; do it slowly.

Fingers and wrist

Technique: With your feet shoulder width apart, raise your hands in front of you. Open your palms to stretch your fingers outwards. Hold that stretch for 3 seconds and then clench the fist tight and hold for 3 seconds. Repeat thrice.

Thereafter, rotate the wrist gently in a circular movement—thrice clockwise and thrice anticlockwise.

Hip rotation

Technique: With your legs roughly shoulder-width apart and keeping your hands on your waist, rotate the hips in a circular movement as if making a big circle using your hips.

Do 3 circles clockwise and 3 anticlockwise

Bending knee—front and back—without support

Technique: These two knee stretches are similar to the knee stretch (page 77) mentioned in the 'Warm-up Exercises 1', except that now you are attempting it without support, so you have to balance yourself on one leg while doing the stretch. If you find

85

this difficult, then do it with support. Try to hold the final position on each leg for 10 seconds in both the front and back stretches.

The entire warm-up routine described so far should take you around 20 minutes.

The warm-up is a very integral part of exercise and we will be using this warm-up sequence a lot in subsequent sections with slight time variations in the *Heating up the Body 1 and 2*.

Attempt these basic yoga postures and stretches

Now that you have loosened up the body and warmed it up well, we will first try a few yoga postures which will help you discover your strengths and weaknesses.

To attempt the following yoga postures, you can put a yoga mat or a dari on the floor. If you want, you can even do these on grass.

Vrikshasana (Tree posture)

Technique: For this balancing posture, stand on one leg—you can use your hands to get your other leg in the position as shown in the picture. Then fold your hands in a namaskar in front of your chest, as shown in the picture. Take your time to find your balance in this position. Fixing your gaze at a point directly in front of you should help you get stable. Once you have found your balance, slowly stretch your hands upward to get into the second position. Try to hold this position for 10 seconds. Then repeat the same while standing on the other leg.

If you find it very difficult to get into this posture, then your balance is not great at present. The other reason for not being able to do this well could also be that either your leg is too stiff and cannot be folded in the position that this posture requires, or that your folded leg keeps slipping. In 'Warm-up Exercises 2', we attempted the knee and ankle stretches balancing on one leg without support. If you found those difficult to execute, then you do need to improve your balance.

Utkatasana variation 1

Technique: Stand with your feet shoulder-width apart and parallel, with the toes pointing forward. Raise your hands high and straight above your head. Now lower your hips by bending your knees slowly, as if you are sitting on an imaginary chair. In the final position, the knees are at a ninety-degree angle, the back is straight, and your hands are stretched and pointing along the direction of your back, as shown in the second picture. Hold that position for a few seconds before you come up. **If you can comfortably hold the final position with knees bent at that angle for more than 15 seconds, then the quadricep mucles of your legs are strong. Otherwise, they need to be strengthened more.**

Shoulder rotation

Technique: We had done shoulder rotation as part of the warm-up stretches. Do the backward rotation of the shoulders again. Try to start with the elbows in position as shown in the first picture. Then take them up and complete a full rotation, bringing them back in a circular movement.

If you feel that the elbows are not going up, making a nice big circle as shown in the pictures, then your shoulders are stiff and need to be opened up to increase their range of movement. Lots of men,

specially the ones who focus too much on strengthening exercises for the shoulders and do not balance it with flexibility exercises, tend to get their shoulders stiff over a period of time—drastically reducing their range of movement.

Sukhasana (Comfortable sitting position)

Technique: Sit cross-legged on the floor. This is a simple, comfortable posture.

If you find it difficult to sit comfortably on the floor then you need to do a lot of stretching exercises to loosen your

leg muscles. If you can sit comfortably but can't straighten your spine completely, then you need to work on your spine to get it more erect.

Paschimottanasa

Technique: Sit on the floor, stretching your legs in front of you. Bend forward and try to touch your hands to your toes.

If you are far from touching your toes then your hamstring muscles, calf muscles, hips, and lower back are stiff. On the other hand, if you can easily wrap your hands around your feet and even touch your forehead to your knees then these mucles are extremely flexible.

Toe towards the forehead stretch

Technique: Sitting with one leg stretched in front of you, pull the other leg towards your chest as shown in the picture. Next, try to bring your toe towards your forehead.

If you are flexible, you should be able to pull the ankle close to your chest easily. Repeat this with the other leg as well.

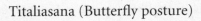

Titaliasana (Butterfly posture)

Technique: Assume the starting position with the soles of your feet together and

pulled in towards you as much as possible. Keep the knees as close to the ground as possible. If your knees are far from the ground then you can use your hands to push them down gently to feel the stretch on the inner thighs. If your knees are touching the ground comfortably, you can stretch your hands forward and bend forward in an attempt to touch your forehead to the ground to feel an increased stretch. Hold the stretch for 6 seconds.

If your knees are far from touching the floor, then your inner thighs are stiff.

Vajrasana

This is an important posture and it is very good for your body if you can sit in it comfortably. **If you can't sit in Vajrasana for up to a minute, then perhaps your ankles need to loosen up more with stretching exercises.**

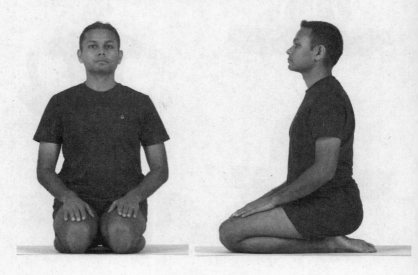

Ardha Naukasana (Half-boat posture)

Technique: Sit in the position shown in the first picture, balancing yourself on the hips with the hands providing slight support. Once you find a balance in that position, raise the hands up and balance, as shown in the second picture. This would require some amount of balance along with contraction of the stomach muscles.

If your stomach muscles are weak, you might find this very difficult.

Utkatasana variation 2

Technique: With your feet roughly shoulder-width apart, slowly squat down completely. In Utkatasana variation 1, you bent your knees half way, as if you were sitting on an imaginary chair. In variation 2, you need to sit all the way down and balance in that position. Join your palms together and stretch them forward to enhance the balance and to keep yourself from rolling backwards.

This is difficult for many people, but is an extremely important posture to master as it is very good for your fitness. **If you are struggling in this position, then your leg muscles, especially the calves, are stiff.**

Bhujangasana (Cobra posture)

Technique: Lie down on your stomach with your palms resting on the floor near your shoulders as shown in the first picture. Now raise your neck and upper body. Use your arms to further raise your upper body and to increase the arch on your back.

You are essentially raising the neck and upper back, and then arching the upper back and the neck, as though you're trying to look back behind you.

If the maximum arch on your back does not look like the 'flexible upper back' picture and looks more like the 'stiff upper back' picture then your upper back needs some work to make it more flexible.

Stiff upper back

Flexible upper back

Shashankasana (Rabbit posture)

After the cobra, move into the rabbit posture.

Technique: Sit back completely, put your forehead on the ground, and stretch your hands straight in front of you.

If you are struggling with this, it could be due to excess weight, stiff ankles, or stiff back and hip muscles.

Plank posture (Holding the push-up starting position)

Technique: This posture is like the starting position of a push-up. The bodyweight should be more on the arms than on the toes. In this posture, the body needs to be parallel to the ground, as shown in the picture, so make sure, you don't raise your hips too much above your shoulders.

If you can't hold this comfortably even for 10 seconds then you need to strengthen your upper body.

Back strengthening variation 1

Technique: Lie down on your stomach with your hands stretched in front of you. Raise your right hand and left leg up as you breathe in. Breathe out as you bring the hand and leg down. Now raise the opposite hand and leg up and then down. Repeat this twice. Each time, try to raise the hand and leg high enough, as shown in the picture.

If this is comfortable for you, then attempt the advanced version of this posture shown below.

Back strengthening variation 2

Technique: From the same starting position as the earlier posture, this time raise both the hands and legs up simultaneously. Keep the elbows and knees straight. Try to hold the final position for 3 to 5 seconds.

Sarpasana (Snake posture)

Technique: Lie down on your stomach with feet together. Put your hands behind you and interlock your fingers. Breathe in as you raise your upper body and neck as much as you can. The attempt should be to raise your upper body till your navel. Hold the final position with the upper body raised for a second and while exhaling, slowly come down to the starting position.

In all these three postures, if you are struggling to raise your body high enough or holding the final position, then your back is either stiff or weak, or both.

Dynamic Paschimottanasana (Dynamic toe touching variation 1)

Technique: Lie down on your back with your hands stretched behind you. Slowly start moving up from that position to

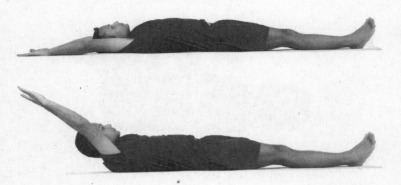

reach your toes as shown in the pictures. Breathe out while coming up to touch your toes. After touching your toes go back slowly while breathing in, and return to the lying down starting position. Do not do this movement with a jerk as you could injure your back. Do not do this movement if you feel too much pain or discomfort while attempting it.

To do this comfortably you need strong core muscles and if you are struggling to do this, you need to strengthen your back and stomach muscles.

Pavanmuktasana

Technique: Lying down on your back, bend both your knees and press them against your stomach with your hands while keeping the fingers interlocked. Hold that position for a few seconds.

This posture will relax your spine which might be good for you after attempting the previous dynamic posture which can be slightly taxing on your lower back. This is a simple posture which everyone should be able to do. **If you are struggling with this one and are not able to fold your knees well, then you really need to include more stretching exercises to improve flexibility.**

Some freehand strength exercises

Push-ups with knee support

Technique: With your hands roughly shoulder-width apart, take the position for push-ups. Put the knees down, as shown in the picture for a slightly easier version of the classic push-ups. Now bend the elbows outward as you lower your body towards the floor and raise it up back to the starting position using your upper-body strength. Cotinue to keep your knees on the ground and attempt a few more push-ups to see how many you can do comfortably and with proper technique. Breathe in when you lower the body and breathe out when you come back up.

Anything less than 5 means poor upper body strength.

Alternatively, you can do push-ups with wall support. Take the support of a short wall or any other firm surface roughly your shoulder height where you can get a firm grip to do push-ups. These are slightly easier but still very beneficial.

Push-ups with a short wall support

Technique: Take support of a short wall or any other firm support at about your shoulder height where you can get a grip. While doing push-ups, make sure your body goes down in one line and comes back up the same way. Many people who have weak arms or do not know the right technique tend to just take their sholulders down and up while the hips stay up. The hips should be lowered when you bend the elbows to do the push-up.

Anything less than 7 means poor upper-body strength.

Squats

Technique: Stand with feet roughly shoulder-width apart  and parallel, as shown in the first picture, and hands stretched in front for balance. Slowly lower the body as if you are about to sit on an imaginary chair. The knees should not protrude too much beyond the toes as you lower the body. Go down to the position shown in the last picture in which the angle at the knees is roughly ninety degrees. Sit on that imaginary chair to the count of 3 and then slowly come back up to the starting position while keeping the knees slightly bent. That is one round of squats.

Do a few rounds as per your present capacity. **Anything less than 5 done comfortably indicates weak lower body and leg muscles, particularly quadriceps.**

On-elbow leg raises

Technique: Lie down on your back while resting on your elbows as shown in the picture and raise both legs close to a ninety-degree angle. Breathe in  as you raise the legs up and try to keep the knees straight as much as possible. Slowly lower the legs towards the floor while breathing out. When your legs are about six inches above the ground raise them again to ninety degrees while breathing in and then again lower them. Repeat raising the legs thrice. If you find it difficult to do it with the breathing at present, then breathe normally while you do it. You can bend the knees slightly while doing this if you feel a strain on your lower back. If you feel a lot of strain on your lower back even

with knees bent, then avoid this as it could over strain your lower back.

To do this effortlessly you need good strength in your lower back and stomach mucles. If you are struggling a lot with these, it indicates weak core muscles.

End the session with Relaxation

Shavasana (Corpse posture)

Technique: Lie down on your back with your hands loose at your side and palms up, and find a comfortable position for Shavasana. Keep your eyes closed and all your muscles absolutely loose. Let the body be absolutely lifeless and still. Even while keeping the muscles loose, be alert and observe yourself—the state of your muscles, the state of your breathing. Watch the state of your mind as an observer and don't pursue any thoughts, just let them pass.

Relax in this possition for about a minute.

Breath awareness with hands on the stomach

Technique: Next, place your hands on your stomach and focus on your breathing. Try to concentrate on your natural breathing without modifying it. Consciously try to notice whether your stomach is moving up and down as you breathe, or is it mostly your chest. In about 30 seconds, slowly roll over to one side and come up to sit in any one of the comfortable seating positions shown below, while maintaining a straight spine.

Vajrasana

or

Sukhasana (Comfortable sitting position)

Sit in Vajrasana or Sukhasana, whichever is more comfortable for you. Keep your spine straight and sit still with your eyes closed for about 30 seconds. Try to be absolutely still.

After about 30 seconds of sitting still, begin taking a few deep breaths. Breathe in slowly to fill your lungs completely and then breathe out very slowly to empty the lungs completely. Try and breathe in to a count of 10 seconds and stretch the exhalation to more than 10 seconds. At this point, as we get ready to end the session, get a stopwatch to time the duration of your exhalation. After breathing in deeply, start the time as you start to exhale. **Try to exhale slowly and steadily, attempting to stretch the exhalation as long as you comfortably can. If it is less than 15 seconds, then you are not breathing very deeply at present.**

Ideally, in Shavasana, you should progressively feel more relaxed rather than growing more impatient over a minute of lying still.

When you place your hands on your stomach to observe your breathing, your stomach should move more as you breathe in and out whereas your chest should stay comparatively still. If the opposite is true for you, then your breathing is shallow. When you sit still with eyes closed, your body should be motionless and your mind should start becoming calmer and move towards stillness.

When you practise deep breathing after sitting still, you should be able to stretch your breathing long enough and feel the lungs getting full with each incoming breath and becoming almost empty with every outgoing breath.

If you find this part of relaxation and breathing very challenging and it makes you restless, then you need to work more towards centring your mind. You will need to practise deep breathing to become calmer and more centred, which will help you be healthier, and allow you to explore your true potential.

Pay Extra Attention to your Weaknesses

After the session, make a note of your strengths and, more importantly, your weaknesses.

Very stiff muscles?

If you find that all your major muscles are stiff in general—you can't touch your toes comfortably or your spine doesn't arch back well in the cobra position—then you need to pay extra attention and give extra time to stretching exercises.

Sometimes you may find that certain parts of your body are flexible while certain others are stiff. You need to pay

extra attention and do specific stretches for those areas that are stiffer.

You must practise the very yoga postures you found yourself struggling in and strive to become better at them with consistent practice. Practise these and other yoga postures and stretching exercises on a regular basis. Do them after doing a basic warm-up (page 76 to 86) as the body will loosen up better and faster when it is warmed up.

Weak muscles?

You might have found that most of your muscles are weak in general, or that some are weaker than others. Attempting

freehand exercises like push-ups, squats, and leg raises must have given you an idea of the current strength of your major muscles. These very exercises and other freehand strength exercises should be focused upon if you need to strengthen your muscles.

Be careful to learn the correct form in the strength exercises before you start to push yourself too much. Push-ups, squats, and other strength exercises done with incorrect technique can injure you rather than making you strong.

Low stamina?

If you struggle to climb four flights of steps at a good pace or get tired brisk walking or running more than a kilometre, which you might have discovered in the warm-up, then you need to work on your stamina. It is a very important aspect of fitness. You might be very strong and very flexible, but will be useless in any sports team if you lack stamina. The good thing is that it is not difficult to build stamina. It just needs some consistent practice.

To build stamina you have to focus more on cardiovascular exercises—exercises that raise your heart rate. To increase your stamina, you have to progressively push yourself beyond your present capacity. If you get tired after three flights of steps presently and feel like resting and catching a breath, push yourself to climb another flight of steps. Walk fast. Leisurely walking will not increase your stamina. And if you can walk or run 1 km at a reasonably fast pace already, try pushing it to 1.5 km and then over time, to 2.5 km.

A stiff spine?

As I discussed in the earlier chapter, it is very important for the spine to be in good condition. I find a lot of people have major stiffness in either the lower or upper back.

Practising most dynamic and static yoga postures in addition to the ones I have explained in the earlier section of dealing with back pain are excellent for the spine.

Though most yoga postures are great for the spine, one posture that I would like to particularly stress on is Bhujangasana or the Cobra posture.

Practise the cobra posture regularly and continue striving to improve the backward-bending arch on your spine each time you practise it.

Restless mind?

If you find it very difficult to sit still or lie down in Shavasana, it might be because your mind is very restless.

You should also practise breath awareness, deep breathing, meditation, prayer, and spend more time in nature to get your mind centred.

Practise Shavasana, sitting in the meditative posture with your spine straight with eyes closed, and deep breathing—like you did for relaxation in the previous section. The more you

practise these, the easier they will become and you will find your mind getting calmer.

Balance?

If you struggled with Vrikshasana (Tree posture) and the knee-bending stretch without support in the warm-up, then your balance needs work. Constantly practising the tree posture along with other balancing postures will improve it.

To begin with, you can take slight support with your hand to help you balance, and then gradually move towards doing it without support. Eventually, the better you get at it, try and hold it for up to a minute without support.

Shallow breathing?

While breathing, you may notice that it is mainly your chest that moves up and down with each inhalation and exhalation, not your stomach. Or you might feel you are unable to stretch your incoming and outgoing breath, or are unable to hold your breath long enough. In this case, you need to focus on breathing exercises that increase your lung capacity and give you better

control over your breathing. You must practise deep breathing techniques and Pranayama (yogic breathing techniques). It is important to practise dynamic yoga postures slowly with total coordination between breathing and movement.

With practice, increase the duration of the incoming and outgoing breath and hold the breath longer when you are holding dynamic postures such as Paschimottanasana (back stretching posture) and even Bhujangasana (cobra posture). These are excellent to improve your breathing as they involve expansion of the chest as you breathe in and contraction of the chest and stomach as you breathe out, resulting in deeper breaths.

Make a One-month Commitment

Mark Your Calendar

Now that you have decided to take charge of your fitness and are armed with the awareness of your strengths and weaknesses in various aspects of fitness, it is time to make a one-month commitment to wake your muscles up and get your body workout ready. You will need to make time for a 20-minute routine, preferably three times, else just two times a week. This one-month routine is a preparation for some fitness 'gems' in the next chapter, get ready for a workout, a sport, or start any exercise routine. Don't worry if you feel this routine is too easy for you, it's just a preparation, so be patient and stick with it.

If you've been regular with some kind of fitness routine and are already fit, then you can shorten this part. I have given a particular set of exercises to be followed each week, raising the bar every successive week. If you are very fit, you could practise the schedule just for a day and move on to the schedule for the next week on your next workout day. This way you will fasten the process for yourself without missing out on the flow that I have intended.

This one-month will focus more on yoga practice, which is part of the process of adopting an 'inside-out' approach to fitness.

This month will require a lot of commitment and regularity. Once you are through this month, your subsequent routine can be much simpler and easier to accommodate into your busy life.

Keep the Basics in Mind

There are a few important things to keep in mind before you undertake any exercise:

- The two to three hours after sunrise and the time around sunset are the best times to exercise. Since you are a busy person, try to exercise in the morning. It's more likely you'll be regular that way. You'll also feel productive and good for the rest of the day.
- Your stomach should be empty, although something light like a fruit is perfectly fine, and in fact good if eaten about half an hour before exercise. After a heavy meal you must wait at least two to three hours before an elaborate exercise routine, though a light walk is fine.
- Wear comfortable clothes and light, proper running or jogging shoes for the brisk walk and jog that we'll be doing

as a warm-up. Unless you have some kind of a dari that you want to use, you will need a yoga mat for the floor exercises—they are available at most sports shops.

- I always recommend going outdoors in fresh air to exercise as much as possible. However, for the short-duration workouts, it might not be practical for you to go to a park nearby. I would advise you to head outdoors for the warm-up jog or brisk walk but stay around your house and come back home for the remaining exercises. Make sure to choose a place in your house where you can open the windows and let in fresh air. Try not to switch on the fan or AC. It's good for you to sweat. Keep water at room temperature nearby and take a few sips whenever needed. If you have a garden close to your house or a balcony, these will be ideal spots for the exercises. You will need a yoga mat or a thick dari for the lying-down exercises and yoga postures.

- If you are starting for the first time, minor discomfort or pain is expected but do not let that deter you. Take good rest. If you continue to feel pain in the muscles from the last session, then avoid strenuous parts of the routine and just stick to gentle walking and focus more on stretches.

- Keep in mind the 'Five Mistakes' I mentioned in the first chapter. Start easy and gentle. It'll require patience, but you will eventually benefit from starting slow. Do not have the 'all-or-nothing approach'. Even if you go off-track and have to miss a few days for some reason, it's okay. Don't abandon it, keep coming back and start a few days before the point you'd left off. Say you were consistent for two weeks and then couldn't continue, repeat the second week and then carry on from there. Missing a day here or there is not a huge problem. You can pick up from where you left off.

Pull Out All Stops

Since you're putting in all the effort, why not also decide to pull out all the stops? Really make a concentrated effort to change your lifestyle.

Over this month, try to incorporate as many of the twenty points from the 'Healthy Habits' in Chapter 1 as you can. Make sure to particularly include the following two points:

- Be active through the day. Find reasons to move rather than not to move. For example, take the stairs instead of the lift.
- Eat a healthy, balanced diet of fresh, natural food. Watch your calories if you want to lose weight.

Choose Your Days for Exercise

Choose your days according to the time commitment you can realistically make for this month. Decide which days of the week that would be—note them on your calendar and mark them as high priority!

20-minute routine: two to three times a week.

Even for the 20-minute exercise routine, keep aside at least half an hour, as you'll take time to wear your shoes, lay down your mat, and prepare for the workout.

Each day of the routine has three parts:

1. Basic warm-up
2. Main exercises for the day
3. Relaxation

Decide whether you want to exercise on Monday, Wednesday, and Friday; or Tuesday, Thursday, and Saturday; or just Tuesday and Thursday. Make sure there is at least a day's gap between two sessions.

If you can only manage to exercise twice a week, then try to have two to three days' gap between the two days' sessions. For example, Tuesday and Friday or Monday and Friday.

If possible, try to go for a brisk walk or a jog over the weekend in addition to the weekday 20-minute routines. After the walk, you could work on your weak areas which you discovered in the earlier chapter, and practise the yoga postures and exercises you've been doing over the week.

On the days you can spare more time, you can increase the duration of the cardio part in the warm-up longer. Also, be active through the week. Apart from the 20-minute routine two to three times a week, do walk and take the stairs whenever you get a chance.

In the 9 minutes that I have allotted for the warm-up and main exercises, I have left room for moving on to the next exercise so you don't have to rush through the exercises.

I have given a simple chart at the back of the book in which you can tick the days you have followed the one-month routine week-wise. The days when you have done just a brisk walk or jog—you should record that as well to keep track of your exercise over the month.

Week One

9 Minutes: Basic warm-up

This warm-up is similar to the 'Basic Warm-up' you did in the earlier section, 'Your Present State' (page 76 to 86). The only difference is that the cardio exercise time duration is reduced in this case.

Heating Up the Body 1

- Wear your running shoes and head out for a walk. Do not go far so you can come back in time to finish the routine. Be around your house or the road outside your house.
- Start by walking at your normal pace for 2 minutes and then increase the pace for 2 minutes.
- Stop for stretches when you've walked for a total of around 4 minutes.

Warm-up Exercises 1

For pictures and technique descriptions see the 'Basic Warm-up', (page 76 to 78)

- Standing toe touching (repeat three times)
- Bending knee—front and back—with support (once on each leg, holding for 5 seconds each)
- Ankle stretch (twice on each leg, hold for 4 seconds each time)
- Ankle rotation (2 times clockwise and 3 times anticlockwise on each leg)

Heating Up the Body 2

- Now get back to the spot you have chosen for exercising. Walk at a very fast pace. If it's comfortable you can even try to jog back lightly. If jogging is not for you, stick to brisk walking.
- If you live on the third or fourth floors, then take the stairs. Even if you are on the ground floor, you can run up and down three flights of stairs before going back into your house.

This last leg of brisk walking or jogging combined with walking up the stairs should be done very fast. You should reach your exercise mat in about a minute. When you stop, your heart rate should have gone up considerably.

Warm-up Exercises 2

For pictures and technique descriptions see the 'Basic Warm-up', (page 79 to 86)

- Side stretches (once on each side, hold the stretch on each side for 10 seconds)
- Side stretch with one hand back (once on each side, hold the stretch on each side for 10 seconds)
- Feet apart forward and backward bend (repeat two times, hold the stretch on each side for 10 seconds)
- Neck stretches (repeat each neck stretch two times, holding it for 3 to 4 seconds on each side)
- Shoulder rotations (three times clockwise and three times anticlockwise)
- Fingers and wrist (open the fingers and clench the fist three times, wrist rotation—three times clockwise and three times anticlockwise)
- Hip rotation (three times clockwise and three times anticlockwise)
- Bending knee—front and back—without support (once on each leg, hold the stretch on each leg for 10 seconds)

9 minutes: Main exercises for the day

This week, we will mainly do yoga postures to gently prepare the body for the next week's exercises. Attempt the following yoga postures in this sequence.

Tadasana variation 1

Technique: Stand with your feet together. Interlock your fingers and stretch your hands upwards above your head. Hold that stretch for a few seconds before you bring your hands down.

Hold the stretch in the final position for 15 seconds.

Tadasana variation 2

Technique: Stand with your feet together, fingers interlocked and stretch your hands above your head like you did for Tadasana variation 1. Now keeping this stretch, bend laterally to your right feeling a nice stretch on one side of your body. Hold that stretch for a few seconds before you come back to the Tadasana variation 1 position. Now keeping the hands in the same position above your head, bend to your left to balance the earlier stretch.

Hold the final stretch for 10 seconds on each side.

Vrikshasana (Tree posture)
Hold the final position for 10 seconds on each leg.

Dynamic Tadasana variation
Technique: Stand with feet parallel, toes pointing straight, and feet shoulder-width apart. Keep your hands on your sides with palms facing inward. While breathing in, slowly start raising your hands upwards and simultaneously start raising your heels to shift weight on your toes with your hands completely stretched upwards over your head in the final position. Hold that position and your breath for a few seconds and then

slowly come back to the starting position while breathing out. Coordinate the breathing and movement perfectly and move very slowly.

Repeat this three times and each time hold the stretched position for 10 seconds.

Vajrasana
Attempt the Vajrasana position on your mat and hold the posture for 20 seconds.

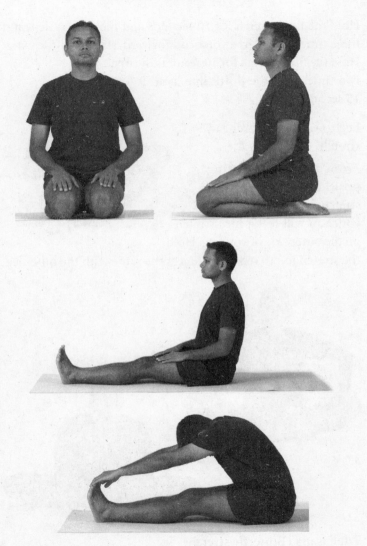

Paschimottanasana (Both legs forward toe touching)

Hold the final stretch for 10 seconds and then relax. Repeat it three times. Each time you bend forward, stretch a little extra. Hold the final stretch for 10 seconds the first two times, and the third time, hold it for 15 seconds.

Leg towards the forehead stretch

From the same starting position as the previous stretch, pull one leg towards you. You will feel a nice stretch on the outer side of your leg. Hold the stretch for 10 seconds. Repeat the same with the other leg.

Titaliasana (Butterfly stretch)

Hold the stretch for 15 seconds.

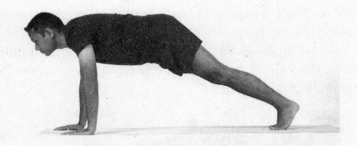

Holding the push-up starting position

Try to hold this position for 15 seconds. If you get tired before that, gently put your knees down to ease the strain on your arms and lie down on your stomach for the next posture.

Bhujangasana (Cobra stretch)

Hold the final cobra position for 10 seconds and then gently come back to the starting position. Breathe in when coming up into the final position and breathe out while coming down to the starting position.

Repeat this three times. Each time, try and stretch a little extra. Hold for 10 seconds for the first two times and for 15 seconds the third time.

Sarpasana (Snake posture)

Repeat this three times. Hold for 6 seconds for the first two times and the third time hold the stretch for 10 seconds.

Shashankasana (Rabbit posture)

After the cobra stretch, put your hips back and relax in Shashankasana, or the rabbit posture for 20 seconds and then lie down on your back for the next dynamic posture.

Lying-down leg raises—single leg

Technique: Lie down on your back with your hands to the side and palms facing down. As you breathe in, raise the left leg up. Try to keep the knee as straight as possible and try to bring the leg at a ninety-degree angle to the body. Hold that position and your breath for 1 second. Breathe out as you lower the leg slowly back to the starting position. Now raise the right leg as you breathe in to repeat the same with the left leg.

Repeat this twice for each leg.

Pavanmuktasana

Relax in this posture for 15 seconds.

2 minutes: Relaxation

Shavasana (Corpse posture)

Lie on your back with hands to the side and palms facing up. Close your eyes and consciously leave all the muscles absolutely loose. Be still in that position with all your focus on your body and your breathing.

Relax in Shavasana for 30 seconds.

Breath awareness with hands on the stomach

Continue to keep your eyes closed and gently place your hands on your stomach. Relax in this position for 30 seconds. Be aware of the slight movement of your stomach as you breathe in and breathe out. To come back, slowly turn your body to the right and come up to sit comfortably.

Sukhasana (Comfortable sitting position)

Sit comfortably with your spine straight, eyes closed, shoulders loose, and forehead relaxed. Be still in this position for 30 seconds and then take 3 deep breaths. Take your time to breathe in slowly through your nose. Fill your lungs completely. Breathe out slowly. Stretch the exhalation as long as you comfortably can. Empty your lungs completely.

If you have a bit more time than the allocated 20 minutes, increase the duration of the walk and jog in the warm-up by a few minutes. Then, increase the repetitions and hold the stretches for longer. You can also increase the time you relax in Shavasana.

Week Two

9 Minutes: Basic warm-up

Same as Week One (page 76 to 86)

9 Minutes: Main exercises for the day

Forward leg raise

We will start the exercises with forward leg raises. These are very good for strengthening and mobilizing the legs and are also a preparatory exercise for martial arts kicks.

Technique: Stand in a balanced position with one leg forward. Raise the leg which is behind and bring it in front of you as high as you comfortably can; then move it back to the starting position. Do not do this with a jerk and don't try and

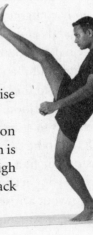

force the leg too high. Raise it to a comfortable height, even if it is just up to your knees at the moment. Repeat the same with the other leg.

Repeat three times with each leg.

Tricep dips

Technique: Find a sturdy chair or a bench about two feet high to do this. Start by sitting on the bench and placing your palms on the sides. Placing your hands right next to your hips, get a grip on the edge of the bench. Now keeping the hands in the same position, plant your feet about one step ahead of the bench with feet shoulder-width apart. From this position, with your hands and feet both roughly shoulder-width apart, your upper body straight, and your body weight evenly distributed on your hands and feet, start lowering the body, bending the elbows. Go down low enough to make a ninety-degree angle at your elbows and then rise up slowly, straightening the elbows to come back to the starting position. This is one repetition.

Attempt 3 to 4 triceps dips. It is difficult to get the technique right for this one at first, so go easy initially. If your technique is wrong or your arms not strong enough, you might find this very difficult. Attempt it, but don't push yourself too far initially.

Squats (page 69 to 70)

Attempt 6 squats. If full squats are difficult for you at the moment, then just go down midway and not all the way down to the final position.

Push-ups with knee support (page 101)

Attempt 6 push-ups.

Push-ups with wall support (page 102)

Alternatively, you can do 6 push-ups with a wall support, which are slightly easier.

Janushirasana (One leg forward toe touching)

Technique: Sit with your right leg stretched in front of you and the left leg bent at the knee, as shown in the picture. Now

stretch your hands towards your right
toe and attempt to take your forehead
towards your right knee. It's fine if
your forehead is not touching
the knee or your hands are not
reaching your toes at present.
The important thing is that
you should be feeling a good

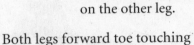

stretch on the hamstrings of
the stretched leg in the final
position.

Hold the final stretch for
10 seconds and

then change the position to repeat
on the other leg.

Both legs forward toe touching
(page 125 to 126)

Hold the final stretch for
10 seconds.

Dynamic Purvottanasana (Dynamic toe touching variation 2)

Technique: Sit comfortably with both your feet stretched in front of you, as shown in the picture. Now reach for your toes in an attempt to touch your fingers to your toes and your forehead to your knees. Breathe out while bending forward in this movement. In a continuous movement, come back to the starting position with your hands touching the ground, turned inward. While breathing in, raise the hips up, as shown in the picture. Hold that position for a second and then come back to the starting position. This is one cycle. This is to

be done as a continuous movement coordinating slow breathing with slow movements.

Attempt 3 cycles.

Shashanka Bhujangasana (Dynamic cobra–rabbit)

Technique: We have practised the cobra (page 61 to 62) and the rabbit posture (page 96) earlier. In the dynamic combination of both, we will do them as a continuous cycle with breath coordination. Lie down on the stomach and take the starting position for cobra with your palms near the shoulders. Breathe in as you raise the upper body in the final position. As you breathe out, take your hips back to sit in the rabbit position. Now as you breathe in, shift your body weight to your hands and flow back into cobra position again. This is one cycle.

Repeat 2 cycles and then lie down on the stomach for the next posture.

Back strengthening variations 1 and 2 (page 97 to 98)

Do the back strengthening variation 1 twice and then variation 2, with both hands and legs up, twice. Breathe in while coming up and breathe out while going down. Each time you come up, hold the position for 5 seconds.

Lying-down leg raises (single leg) (page 129)

Do this twice on each leg.

Lying-down leg raise (both legs)

Technique: Lie down on your back with hands to the side and palms facing down. As you breathe in, raise both legs up slowly. Try to keep the knees as straight as possible and try to make a ninety-degree angle between the legs and the upper body. Hold that position and your breath for 1 second.  Breathe out as you lower the legs slowly back to the starting position. If it is difficult at the moment, you can bend the knees slightly. If it's still very difficult then just repeat the previous version, raising one leg at a time.

Repeat this 3 times.

Dynamic toe touching variation 1 (page 98 to 99)

Repeat 4 to 5 times. Avoid coming up with a jerk as it could injure your lower back.

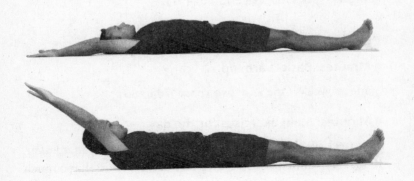

Pavanmuktasana (page 60)

Relax in Pavanmuktasana for 30 seconds.

2 Minutes: Relaxation.

Same as Week One (page 130 to 131).

Week Three

9 Minutes: Basic warm-up

Same as Weeks One and Two (page 76 to 86).

9 Minutes: Main exercises for the day

This week we shall attempt the very important Suryanamaskar. If this is too difficult for you then do not exert yourself too much and be gentle. Skip or modify the steps that are too difficult for you at present. If your spine is weak or in pain, then go easy in the forward-bending movements or avoid them altogether for now. Do not do any movement with a jerk. Though I have given the correct breathing to go with every step, do not worry about the breathing initially. First get the basic flow of the different postures in Suryanamaskar and then incorporate the breathing with movements.

Suryanamaskar (One cycle)

Technique:

Starting position: Stand at the front of your mat, with your feet together and your hands folded in a namaskar in front of your chest.

Position 1: While breathing in, stretch your hands upwards. Arch back and tilt your neck back with your hands and ears roughly in one line.

Position 2: From position 1, bend forward while breathing out. Touch your toes and attempt to take your forehead towards your knees.

Position 3: Put your palms on the mat, shoulder-width apart, right next to either leg as you bend your knees. Now take your left leg back completely. With your body weight equally distributed on both palms, the front foot flat on the mat, and the back foot with its toes turned in and knee slightly touching the ground—raise the neck and upper body, tilting the neck back as much as possible, attempting to increase the arch in the upper back. Breathe in while raising the neck and upper body in this position.

Position 4: From position 3, take your right leg behind to join the left one to get into a position similar to the push-up posture. Your body weight should be largely on your arms and a bit on the toes that are turned in. Do not raise your hips too high.

Positions 5a and 5b: From position 4, bring your knees down on the mat and then lower your upper body like you would do in a push-up. Exhale while going down. If your arms are weak at present, you can rest your chest on the mat completely when you go down. Else, using your arm strength, hold the position where your chest is almost touching the mat but not completely resting on it.

Position 6: From position 5b, you now have to come up into the cobra position while breathing in. You have to come up in a way that you make an arc moving  forward and then upward into the final cobra position with the neck and upper body raised. In the cobra position your ankle is open, with the toes not turned in. If your arms are strong and if

you choose to not put your chest down completely in position 5b, the movement to come into the cobra should be first moving forward and then upwards, forming an arc. Doing this with grace requires good arm strength. If you are not able to do this

too well at the moment, then do it with the earlier method of resting the chest completely on the mat for now, till you build better upper body strength over a period of time by doing push-ups.

Position 7: From position 6, raise the hips upwards, keeping the palms in the same position. Breathe out while lifting the hips. Keep the knees as straight as possible and push the heels towards the mat. You will feel a good stretch on your calves. Keep the upper

back pushed in as much as possible. Your body should be in the shape of a mountain, something which is explained in the name of this posture as well—Parvatasana.

Position 8: From position 7, bring your left leg forward next to your left hand—make sure that the leg is on the inside of the hand—while raising your neck and upper body, creating an

upward arc. Breathe in while raising the neck and upper body. This position is similar to position 3 with only the leg positions switched.

Position 9: From position 8, bring the right leg in front as well and straighten your knees to come to a standing toe-touching position. Breathe out while getting into this position, which is similar to position 2.

Position 10: From position 9, breathe in as you come up to a standing position and stretch your hands and neck upwards, getting into the same posture as position 1.

This completes one cycle of the Suryanamaskar. You are now ready to go back to position 2 to start another cycle.

Attempt 3 cycles of Suryanamaskars at your own pace.

After the Suryanamaskar, relax with the following stretches.

Janushirasana (Forward one leg toe touching) (page 134 to 135)
Hold the stretch for 10 seconds on each leg.

Sideways single-leg toe touching

Technique: While facing straight ahead, stretch your right leg to the side. Bend the knee of the left leg with toes facing inwards in the direction of the right leg. This is the starting position, as shown in the picture. Now continue facing straight in front of you, stretch your right hand sideways to touch your right toe. At the same time stretch your left hand in the direction of your stretched right leg from over your head, as shown in the picture. Hold for a few seconds feeling a good stretch on the inner thigh of the right leg as well as the left side of your body. After holding the stretch for a few seconds, repeat the same on the other side with the left leg stretched outward.

Hold this stretch for 10 seconds on each side.

Ardha Naukasana (Half boat posture) (page 93)
Hold the final position for up to 15 seconds.

Half Camel posture

Technique: Sit on your knees, as shown in the picture with your toes turned inward. With your right hand, take the support of your right heel and raise the stomach up while increasing the arch on your back and

stretching the left hand back, as shown in the picture. Hold the stretch for a few seconds and come back very slowly to the starting position. Now repeat the same with the left hand supported on the left heel.

Hold the stretch for 10 seconds with each hand.

If the half camel posture is too difficult for you, then do the 'On knees backward bend', with the hands on hips as shown in the picture.

On-knees backward bend

Hold the stretch for 20 seconds.

At this point, practise 3 more cycles of the Suryanamaskar.

Breath awareness with hands on the stomach (page 106)

After the Suryanamaskar, relax in this lying down position with your hands on your stomach for 15 seconds.

Merudandasana (Lying down spinal twist)

Technique: Lying down on your back, stretch both hands to the sides, as shown in the starting position. Now bend the right knee and place the right foot just above your left knee. With your left hand, push your right knee to your left side, attempting to touch your knee to the ground, and turn your head to the right. You will feel a good stretch on your lower back. Hold this position for a few seconds and then come back to the starting position. Now do the same stretch on the other side, bending your left leg

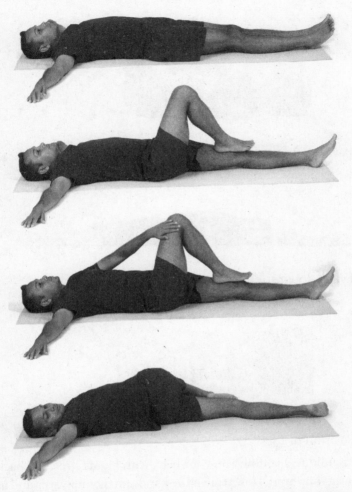

this time and taking it to your right with the help of the right hand, while moving your head to the left.

Hold the twist for 10 seconds on each side. Repeat two times on each side.

Pavanmuktasana (page 60)
Relax in this posture for 20 seconds.

Lying-down stretching body tall

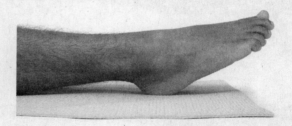

Position of toes

Technique: Lie down on your back with hands stretched back over your head. Now stretch the hands further upwards and at the same time, push your toes downwards. Attempt to make your body as 'tall' as possible, stretching it as much as you can. Hold that position for a few seconds, then relax, leaving all the muscles loose.

2 Minutes: Relaxation

Same as Weeks One and Two (page 130 to 131)

Week Four

9 Minutes: Basic warm-up

Same as last week (page 76 to 86)

9 Minutes: Main exercises for the day

Suryanamaskar (page 141 to 145)

Begin the main exercises with 2 cycles of the Suryanamaskar.

Virabhadrasana (Warrior posture)

Technique: Take a big step forward with your right leg. Make sure that the legs are not in the same line and your right foot is at least four inches to the right of your left foot. The angle at

the knee of your front leg should be almost ninety degrees.. Now stretch both your hands up, as shown in the starting position and try to find your balance in this position. Once you find a good balance with your hands stretched upwards, arch your back, taking your hands and the neck back. This back bend should create a nice stretch and arch in your upper back. Hold that position, balancing there for a few seconds. Now come back to the starting position, bring your leg back and repeat the same, taking the left leg forward. Breathe in when you arch back in the final position and breathe out when you come back to the starting position.

Hold for 10 seconds in the final position. Do it once with the right leg forward and then with the left leg forward.

Front kick

Technique: Stand comfortably with your left leg forward. Now lift your right foot and raise your knee as high as possible without losing balance. Immediately straighten the knee to launch a straight kick in front of you and then bring the leg back to the starting position.

This entire movement is fast and continuous, right from raising the knee up to kicking and bringing the leg back to starting position. But be careful to avoid jerking. It should be a gentle graceful movement. To kick with the left leg, stand with your left leg back and right forward in the starting position.

Kick three times with one leg and then three times with the other leg.

Straight punches

Technique: Stand with one leg forward, knees slightly bent, fists tight, hands up near your face, and shoulders loose. The toe of the front leg should be facing straight and the back leg should be slightly outwards. Punch with your right hand, stretching it in one straight line and quickly bring it back along the same line. Now punch with your left hand, straightening it completely and then bringing it back along the same line to the starting position. Initially, do the movement slowly, and then you can throw faster punches as you get more perfect in the movement. Throw 4 punches and then pause for a second before throwing another 4.

You might find it awkward if you have not done this before. Watching a good boxing movie like *Rocky, Cindrella Man,* or *Million Dollar Baby* might help!

Practise a few punches for 30 seconds with small breaks in between.

Tricep dips (page 132)

Attempt 4 to 6 tricep dips or according to your capacity. Go easy if you feel your technique is not right.

Squats (page 69 to 70)

Attempt 6 to 8 squats.

Dynamic toe touching variation 1 (page 98 to 99)

Repeat 4 times. Only if this is very comfortable then try the more challenging variation.

Dynamic toe touching variation 1—Challenging version 1

Technique: The technique is similar to the 'Lying-down toe touching variation 1'. In this more challenging variation, as you raise your upper body, simultaneously raise the knees to come up and balance in the half boat position (page 93) for a fraction of a second before you lower your body again. Breathe out when you come up in the half boat posture and breathe in as you go back. Don't do this with a jerk or if your back hurts while doing it.

Repeat 4 times.

If you find this one very difficult, then avoid it. You can repeat the earlier easier version or the lying-down leg raises instead (page 129) to strengthen your core muscles more.

Marjari asana (Cat stretch)

Technique: Place your knees and hands on the mat, as shown in the picture. As you breathe out, tuck the neck inwards,

pulling the stomach in, and push your spine upwards; you will get a good stretch on your spine. Pause in that position for a second and as you breathe in, push the stomach down while simultaneously raising the neck up to feel a gentle stretch on the neck and upper back. This is one cycle.

Practise 3 cycles of the cat stretch.

Vyagrasana (Tiger stretch)

Variation 1

Technique: The starting position is same as that of the cat stretch. As you breathe out, lift the left knee and bring it towards the stomach and simultaneously tuck the neck inwards as if you are attempting to move your knee and nose closer to each other. Pause in this position for a fraction of a second and then, as

you breathe in, raise the neck up and the leg up with the knee slightly bent and the toes facing upwards, towards the ceiling. Pause in this position for a second and then again tuck the neck in and the knee in as you did before. This is one cycle.

Repeat the Tiger stretch variation two times on each leg.

Tiger stretch variation 2

Technique: Tiger stretch variation 2 is very similar to variation 1, the only difference being that the knee of the raised leg is kept straight instead of bent.

Repeat two times on each leg.

Shashankasana (Rabbit posture) (page 96)
Relax in the rabbit posture for 15 seconds.

Push-ups with knee support (page 101)
OR

Push-ups using wall support
(page 102)
Do either of these push-up variations.
Attempt 6 to 8 repetitions.

Hands behind the neck leg raises
Technique: This is similar to the
lying-down leg raises (page 129). In
the starting position, lie down on
your back with your feet together,
toes pointing straight, and your

hands interlocked behind your neck. Raise the neck and upper back slightly to feel a slight contraction on your stomach. Now raise both the legs up together to a ninety-degree angle while breathing out and then lower the legs slowly while breathing in. Do not touch the floor completely. Take your legs up again for the next cycle while breathing out. While doing this, do not pull your neck up with your hands. To avoid straining the neck make sure you are looking up straight at the ceiling. If you find this very tough or you feel a strain on your lower back, then bend your knees slightly while doing this. If it is still too difficult then do the 'Single leg lying-down leg raises' (page 129) instead.

Repeat four times.

Crunches

Technique: Lie down on your back and bend your knees at a ninety-degree angle. Interlock your feet and your hands behind your neck. As you breathe out, raise your neck and upper back slightly to feel a contraction (crunch) on the stomach. Pause in this position for a fraction of a second, feeling that contraction. Breathe in as you return to the starting position. This is one crunch.

You might not feel much of a contraction on the stomach muscles for the first few crunches but avoid pulling the neck up too much with your hands as that might strain your neck instead of working on your stomach. After a few crunches, you will start to feel a nice strain on your stomach muscles. At that point, do a few more to increase the contraction on the stomach before you relax. Crunches are a great way to strengthen your stomach muscles without straining your back. Keep looking up at the ceiling throughout the movement to make sure you are not pulling your neck unnecessarily.

Attempt 10 crunches.

Setubandhasana (Bridge posture)

Technique: Lie down comfortably on your back. Bend the knees with the feet placed on the mat, maintaining a comfortable shoulder-width distance between the legs. Your hands should be by your side, with palms facing down. The position should be such that you could easily hold your ankle with your hands. Now keeping the palms down, raise the stomach up as much as you can while breathing in. The body weight should shift more to your shoulders as you try to create a nice arch on your back with the knees almost at a ninety-degree angle. Hold that position for a second and then bring your hips down while breathing out. This is one cycle.

Do 3 cycles of Setubandhasana. In the third cycle, try to hold for 10 seconds or more without holding your breath.

Pavanmuktasana (page 60)

Hold for 10 seconds.

2 Minutes: Relaxation

Same as last week (page 130 to 131).

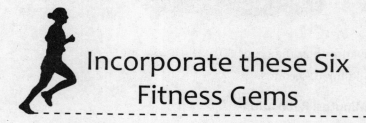

Incorporate these Six Fitness Gems

Throughout school and college, I was seriously into sports and was constantly competing in national-level martial arts tournaments. After winning medals in consecutive inter-collegiate tournaments and being selected for the prestigious University of Delhi boxing team, I did not do any elaborate workout or play any sport for three years after college. I got busy with life and chalking out a career, leaving sports behind, as so many of us do.

Even though I was not doing any regular workouts, I retained my basic fitness and was easily able to get back to my previous fitness level. Even after a three-year gap, I was soon able to participate in martial arts competitions.

The reason I was able to do this was because I decided to follow the advice of one of my fitness teachers, and one of the fittest people I have ever met, Mr Premamay Biswas. He was with the Indian railways and had been coaching national-level swimmers. He had come to our school for two months as a visiting fitness coach. At that time, I used to be the boxing captain of my school and was very dedicated to fitness. He was not only a great swimmer but a great gymnast, martial artist, yoga and fitness expert, and was ten times fitter than me, even at 50. I made him my guru and for two months I spent most of my time with him, even bunking classes, to learn the nuances of fitness. Though I have trained under many great fitness teachers, what I learnt under his guidance has had a lot of influence on my approach to fitness and what I teach.

Apart from teaching me many elaborate fitness and martial arts techniques, he also taught me a few gems.

That's exactly what he called them. He said, 'I am giving you a few gems and come what may, do these religiously, like brushing your teeth.' He taught me a few very simple things which would take me just a few minutes every day and were nothing close to the high-intensity, elaborate workouts I was used to doing. One of the gems he taught me was a series of a few simple stretches I was supposed to do first thing in the morning for all of three minutes. He told me that I could even do them right on the bed the moment I woke up!

In those days, my highly elaborate and regular workouts used to last over an hour. I wondered why he wanted me to do those simple things, but I did them anyway. I did them every day thereafter.

That was more than eighteen years back and even now, whether I am travelling, and irrespective of whether I am able to do my regular elaborate workouts or not, I do my wake-up stretches for a few minutes after getting up. They have made a huge difference to my life in all spheres, including my creativity and especially my health, fitness, and wellness.

What I want to share with you is my own variation of his precious gems—variations that I have evolved over the years based on the original stretches that he taught me. I make sure I teach the wake-up stretches to whoever I train. These are often slightly modified to suit every individual. I advise them to do the wake-up stretches regularly, every day, even if they are not able to do the rest of the elaborate workouts.

There are a few positions, particularly the cat stretch and cobra stretch, done in particular sequence which is integral to these wake-up stretches.

I had once gone for a workout to Joggers Park in Bandra, Mumbai with my friend Arti who has been designing my holistic, breathable clothes for years.

It was late evening so the light was dim. As we were walking, I saw someone doing stretches that looked very similar to the wake-up stretches sequence I make all my students do. I knew it had to be someone I trained at some point and felt happy that they were doing those stretches with such focus and grace. It was a lean, athletic, tall boy. On our next round, out of curiosity, without disturbing the person, I went a little closer and found that it was none other than Ranbir Kapoor.

We had done some extensive sessions while he was preparing for his debut film. Our sessions were more focused on yoga, stretching, and mind centring—as it complemented the strength training he was doing for his fitness. Since he was busy shooting for his film at the time, our sessions were a bit erratic, and it had been a long time since we'd done our last session. That was all the more reason why I was happy to see him doing the stretches so beautifully on his own.

Ranbir is a fantastic football player with good all-round fitness, but even a vigorous sport like soccer does not ensure the perfect well-being of the spine. The wake-up stretches, which predominantly involve opening up the spine, complement a sport or any other form of workout beautifully. They are not only meant for someone who is pressed for time—even a fit sportsperson would benefit immensely from them.

Now that you have woken up your muscles and joints with the one-month commitment, it is time for you to incorporate the wake-up stretches and the five other 'Gems' that you have prepared your body for over the last one month. Make these a part of your life.

Gem # One

Wake-Up Stretches

Do the wake-up stretches soon after getting up in the morning; you can even do them right on your bed. If your mattress is too soft for you to do the stretches properly, then do them on a yoga mat or dari. Do not rush through the stretches. Take your time to hold each stretch and to move from one position to the next.

Variation A: 2 minutes

Sit comfortably in Vajrasana(page 92) or Sukhasana (comfortable sitting position) and take two deep breaths. Stretch the outgoing breath much longer than the incoming

breath. For the next few stretches you can continue to sit in Vajrasana or Sukhasana.

Gently stretch the neck backwards, hold that stretch for 10 seconds and then stretch the neck downwards and

hold for 5 seconds. Repeat this two times. The backward bend of the neck is held a little longer than the forward bend.

Hand position

Interlock the fingers and stretch your hands upwards, feeling a good stretch on your spine in the final position. Hold the stretch for 10 seconds before

you bring the hands down. Repeat this two times. The second time, try to stretch more and hold it longer.

Hand position

Put your hands back with the fingers touching the mat. Now pull the shoulders back and simultaneously tilt the neck

back as if you are trying to look back behind you. In the final position you should be feeling a nice gentle stretch on your neck and shoulders. Hold that stretch for 10 seconds before coming back to the starting position.

Marjari asana (Cat stretch) (page 159 to 160)

Repeat the cat stretch twice. Breathe out when you pull the spine up and breathe in when you push the stomach down. If you wish to hold a stretch for a little longer, then breathe normally while holding that stretch.

Bhujangasana (Cobra Stretch) (page 61 to 62)

Do the Bhujangasana thrice. Do it slowly. Breathe in when you come up. Hold the stretch for a second. Breathe out when you come down. The third time when you come up, breathe normally while holding the final position. Try to hold this position for about 10 seconds. It will prepare your spine and enable you to have an alert and energetic day ahead.

Shashankasana (Rabbit posture) (page 96)

Relax in the rabbit posture for 10 seconds.

Sit up after the rabbit posture. Keep your spine erect, close your eyes and be still in that position for 10 seconds.

Hand position

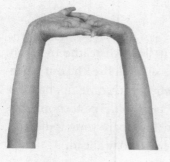

Interlock your fingers and stretch your hands up to end your wake-up stretches and start your day on a great note.

Variation B: 4 minutes

Sit comfortably in Vajrasana or Sukhasana (comfortable sitting position) (page 92, 89 to 90) and take two deep breaths. Stretch the outgoing breath much longer than the incoming breath.

For the next few stretches, you can continue to sit in Vajrasana or Sukhasana. In this version of the wake-up stretches, the initial few stretches are shown sitting in Vajrasana. If you would prefer to do these sitting in Sukhasana (comfortable sitting position), you can do so.

Gently stretch the neck backwards,

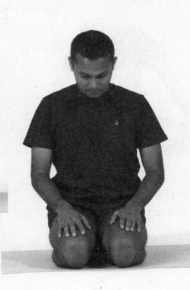

hold that stretch for 10 seconds and then stretch the neck downwards and hold for 5 seconds. Repeat this two times. Hold the backward stretch a little longer. Interlock the fingers and stretch your hands upwards, feeling a good stretch on your spine in the final position. Hold the stretch for 10 seconds before you bring the hands down.

Repeat this two times. Try to stretch

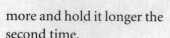

more and hold it longer the second time.

To twist to your left, take your left hand back and turn your neck and shoulders to your left as much as you can. Take help from your right hand to get an extra stretch. Repeat the same with a twist to your right. Hold the twist for 5 seconds on each side.

Put your hands back with the fingers touching the mat. Now pull the shoulders back and simultaneously tilt the neck back as if you are trying to look back behind you. In the final position you should feel a nice gentle stretch on your neck and shoulders. Hold that stretch for 10 seconds before coming back to the starting position.

Paschimottanasana (Both legs forward toe touching) (page 125 to 126)

Hold the stretch for 3 seconds.

Marjari asana (Cat stretch) (page 159 to 160)

Repeat the cat stretch two times. Breathe out when you push the spine up and breathe in when you push the stomach down. If you wish to hold the stretch for longer then breathe normally while holding the stretch.

Calf stretch

After you finish the cat stretch, stretch one leg back from the same position, straightening the knee. Resting the stretched leg on its toes, push the heel of the foot back to feel a stretch on the calf muscle of that leg. Hold that calf stretch for 5 seconds and then bring this leg back to the starting position. Now do the same stretch on the other leg. Repeat this stretch twice on each leg and hold the stretch for 5 seconds each time.

Upper back stretch

After the calf stretch, come back to the cat stretch position. From the cat stretch position, keeping the knees in the same ninety-degree position, stretch your hands forward and press the upper back downwards towards the ground. Raise the neck up slightly. You feel a distinct stretch on your upper back. Hold the stretch for 15 seconds and then get back into the cat position for the next stretch.

Vyagharasana (Tiger stretch variation 1) (page 161 to 162)

Do the tiger stretch twice on each leg. Breathe out when you bend the knee in and breathe in when you raise the leg up. After you finish the Tiger stretch, come on your elbows and lie on your stomach for the next stretch.

Bhujangasana (Cobra Stretch) (page 61 to 62)

Do the cobra stretch thrice. Breathe in as you raise your neck and upper body and breathe out as you come back to the starting position. In each successive round, stretch a little more and hold the stretch for a little longer. The third time you come up in the final cobra position, hold the stretch longer while breathing normally. You can hold the stretch for up to 15 seconds. It will enhance your energy and alertness through the day.

Shashankasana (Rabbit posture)
(page 96)

After the cobra,
relax in
rabbit
posture for 10 seconds.

After the rabbit posture, slowly come
up and sit up comfortably in Vajrasana
(page 92) or Sukhasana (page 89 to 90)
(comfortable sitting position).

Sit still

Sit still for 10 seconds with your
eyes closed.

Backward neck bend

Stretch your neck backwards and
hold it there for 10 seconds.

Interlock and stretch hands up

Hand position

Interlock your hands and stretch them upwards. Raise the neck up slightly as you stretch.

Deep breaths

Take 3 deep breaths.

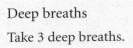

Rubbing palms

Rub both palms against each other for about 10 seconds. Once you feel a little heat in the palms, immediately put them on the

eyes for 5 seconds and bring them down to the rest of your face for 5 seconds. Repeat two times. Once your face absorbs that positive energy, you are ready to start your day on a perfect note.

Gem # Two

Suryanamaskar

It takes a long time to be able to truly master the Suryanamaskar. At near perfection, the movements should be slow, gentle, fluid, and graceful, almost like a dance, with perfect breath coordination. There should be a pause at each position coinciding with the pause in breathing. In that pause, there should be complete stillness in the body and mind. Neither should be wavering. You must strive to master the Suryanamaskar by practising it every day if possible.

Once you have near mastered it, never let your technique slide back, practise constantly. Practise it after your wake-up stretches in the morning when you have the time. Practise it after your walk. Practise it when you are holidaying at a nice resort. Practise it after you get back from work after sitting at the desk the whole day. Just a few cycles of the Suryanamaskar, which only take a few minutes, will activate all your muscles head to toe and give you immense health benefits.

Though I have explained the technique earlier (page 141 to 145), you should get your technique checked and corrected by an expert. Teachers from different styles of yoga practise have slightly different versions of the Suryanamaskar and its not like one is correct and the other incorrect, as long as the basic essence remains the same.

Once you get a good rhythm following the technique described in the earlier chapter, you can add another aspect to it. In the technique described, if you keep the right leg forward in position three, then you are bringing the left leg forward in position eight of the same cycle. Now in the next cycle begin with keeping the left leg forward in position three and bring

the right leg forward in position eight. So basically, whichever leg is forward in position eight of the previous cycle will be kept forward in position three of the next cycle. This will create a better balance. I suggest you start this only when you have reasonably mastered the positions and developed a flow in them else incorporating this right in beginning might make it confusing for you.

Unless you've been very regularly doing it, do a little walk or climb a few steps to warm up the body before practising the Suryanamaskar. If your lower back or neck is in pain, go easy on the forward-bending movements.

Gem # Three

Your Cardio

Cardiovascular exercise is extremely essential as it exercises the most important muscle in your body—your heart. You can create a muscular, chiselled physique by just doing anaerobic exercises without doing much cardio exercise, but you do so at the risk of leaving your main and most useful muscle weak, while surrounding it by strong muscles.

Cardio exercises raise your heart rate, improve blood circulation, raise your meta-bolic rate, and strengthen your heart, among many other benefits. It is the most important aspect of fitness and should be given top priority.

You should have three to four of your own ways of including a cardio exercise in both your day-to-day activities and your workout.

So find your cardio activity and master what

you are not good at presently. Brisk walking, jogging, running, skipping, cycling, certain kinds of dancing, stair climbing, climbing an uphill slope, shadow boxing, spot jogging, swimming, or playing any sport are all great cardio-based activities. Remember, it is those activities that get your heart pacing faster and get you a bit out of breath. Choose the ones that suit you best, do them frequently and use your cardio to get a little breathless every day.

Gem # Four

Static and Dynamic Postures

These are some simple yet important yoga postures. You have already tried most of these postures earlier in this chapter. You must strive to master all of these.

Some might be easier for you, some difficult. Practise all of them once in a while to retain your mastery and to attain perfection in the postures you're still struggling with. They might look very simple but have tremendous benefits to your health, fitness, and well-being.

Static postures

Mastery over a static posture means that it should have good form, be graceful, be unwavering, and you should be able to hold it for as long as you want. While holding a posture for long, your breathing should be deep and slow. When you hold the posture with total awareness of the body and the breath, you will realize that each posture has a specific effect on your breathing and the subtle energy flow in the body.

Vrikshasana (Tree posture) (page 87)

Virbhadrasana
(Warrior posture)
(page 154 to 155)

Bhujangasana
(Cobra posture)
(page 61 to 62)

Shashankasana
(Rabbit posture)
(page 96)

Vajrasana (page 92)

Janushirasana (One leg forward toe touching) (page 134 to 135)

Tadasana (Palm tree posture) (page 123 to 124)

Technique: You can go a little further from the easier technique described earlier and raise your heels to shift weight to your toes. Balance on your toes in this final Tadasana position.

Trikonasana (Triangle posture)

Technique: The technique for Trikonasana is the

same as the 'Side stretch' (page 79 to 80) that we did in the warm-up. When doing the same as a yoga posture, move with more awareness of your body as well as breathing and hold the stretch for longer.

Ustrasana (Half and full camel posture) (page 147 to 148)

Only if you are very comfortable doing the half camel posture, you should try the full camel posture.

Technique: To get into the full camel posture, start with sitting on your knees and toes turned in, like you did for the half camel. Get your right hand back and let it rest on your right heel. Now take your left hand and similarly rest it holding your left heel. Push your stomach up and tilt your neck back to get into the final full

camel position. Hold that position for a few seconds according to your capacity. To come back, leave one hand first and then gently bring your body and the other hand to come out of the posture.

Titaliasana (Butterfly posture) (page 91 to 92)

Merudandasana (Spinal twist) (page 148 to 149)

Ardha Naukasana (Boat posture) (page 93)

Vipreet Naukasana (Reverse boat posture) (page 67 to 68)

Sarpasana (Snake posture) (page 98)

Setubandhasana (Bridge posture) (page 166 to 167)

Pavanmuktasana (page 60)

Shavasana (Corpse posture) (page 58 to 59)

Dynamic postures

In dynamic postures, there should be slow, rythmic, and graceful movements with perfect coordination between the breathing and movement. Inhalation and exhalation should be deep and slow. The movement and breathing should be totally coordinated so that when the movement is paused, breathing should also pause. When the movement resumes after the pause, breathing should also resume with it.

Dynamic Tadasana variation
(page 123 to 124)

Dynamic Padahastasana (Standing toe touching) (page 77)

Dynamic Paschimottanasana (Dynamic toe touching Variation 1) (page 98 to 99)

Marjari asana (Cat stretch) (page 159 to 160)

Vyaghrasana (Tiger stretch) (page 161 to 162)

Dynamic Purvottanasana (Dynamic toe touching Variation 2) (page 136 to 137)

Dynamic Shashank–Bhujangasana (Dynamic cobra–rabbit) (page 137 to 138)

Gem # Five

Deep Breathing and Anytime, Anywhere Stretches

In Chapter 2, I have discussed the immense importance of correct and deep breathing. You should practise taking a few deep breaths every morning with the wake-up stretches.

Make deep breathing an integral part of your life. Our world is becoming more chaotic; our lives more sedentary and stressful by the day. It is essential to counter the ill effects of our modern lifestyle by breathing deeply.

Make it a point to take 3 deep breaths:
- Soon after you wake up
- Before starting to eat breakfast, lunch, or dinner
- Before you sleep at night

Whenever you find yourself getting stressed, angry, or nervous—just take a few deep breaths. Once your breathing rate slows down, the mind will have no choice but to relax.

If you live in a large metropolis, like I do, you'll realize that it is difficult to get fresh air. When you do get the chance to be in fresh air, make sure to take a few deep breaths to replenish the stale air in your lungs.

Like I mentioned earlier, in taking a deep breath, the key is to exhale completely. Exhale softly, yet steadily, while stretching the duration of exhalation as long as comfortably possible. With practise, you should try to be able to exhale for up to 30 seconds or more over a period of time.

Apart from deep breathing, practise these simple stretches few times a day or as often as you can. These stretches will counter the postural imbalance that our modern, sedentary lifestyle is leading us to at a very fast rate. You can practise deep breathing and these following stretches anywhere throughout the day—in the office, on an airplane, or whenever you feel the need to stretch out and relax.

Sitting traction exercise 1
(page 137)

Traction exercise 2 (page 69 to 70)

Sitting—shoulders and neck back stretch (page 63)

Standing—shoulders and neck
back stretch (page 63 to 64)

Standing backward bend
(page 62)

Gem # Six

Freehand Strength Exercises

Along with the previous five gems—Wake-up stretches, Suryanamaskar, Cardio, Yoga postures, and Deep breathing and anytime, anywhere stretches—you should incorporate these basic and extremely important freehand exercises in your life and practise them constantly. Whenever you manage to go for a brisk walk, you can follow it up with these exercises. You must first work towards perfecting the techniques of these exercises and then practise a few repetitions on a regular basis. Practising these will make sure that you will keep up a good level of fitness and be ready to start any workout regimen, take up a sport, or any other physically challenging activity. I am listing some of the important freehand exercises—you have already practised these in your one-month routine.

Basic warm-up

The basic warm-up (page 76 to 86) that we have been practising is extremely useful and should be done before taking on any strenuous exercise or activity. While the warm-up exercises prevent injury and improve the range of movement in preparation for more strenuous exercises— these stretches and rotations in themselves are also great to activate all the muscles in the body, mobilize joints, and improve flexibility.

Push-ups

You can choose to do push-ups with knee support (page 101) or with wall support (page 102). If these are very easy for you, then you can attempt the advanced push-ups (page 227) described in the next chapter.

Squats (page 69 to 70)

Tricep dips (page 132 to 133)

Back strengthening variations 1 and 2 (page 97 to 98)

Crunches (page 165)

Hands behind the neck leg raises (page 163 to 164)

Dynamic toe touching variation 1 challenging version 1 (page 159)

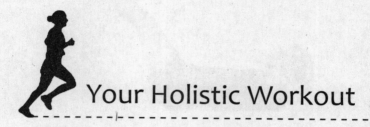

Your Holistic Workout

I have incorporated most of the exercises given in the six gems within the workout routine that I will be describing in this chapter. Apart from your workouts, practise the six gems whenever possible, so you attain perfection in them. Never let your technique slide back due to lack of consistent practice.

Basics of a Workout

Throughout the previous chapters, I have stressed on the importance of being physically active. In the last chapter, we got the body moving to learn some basic yoga postures and freehand cardio, strength, and flexibility exercises.

Doing gentle yoga stretches, taking the stairs instead of the lift, or going for a brisk walk well within the comfort levels of your body is great and extremely beneficial for you.

But, it does not entirely qualify as a workout.

A workout involves pushing the fitness capacity of your body beyond its current capability.

For someone who's just beginning, trying to jog or attempting the Suryanamaskar might feel very difficult. It could qualify as pushing the body beyond its present capacity, and it can arguably qualify as a workout for that person. For a fitter person used to working out, a few Suryanamaskars or a short jog are effortless and won't constitute a workout, although it'll still be great for both their fitness and well-being. For someone who is very frail, weak or older, climbing a few flights of steps could be a workout. Running 3 km might be easy and enjoyable for one person and an intense workout for another.

So what constitutes a workout depends on your own personal fitness level and capacity.

It's not that high-intensity workouts are superior to just brisk walking or doing yoga and lighter exercises. They are all different and have different kinds of benefits.

Ideally, we should incorporate gentle yoga stretches, walking, and breathing exercises into our lifestyle, and along with that, do intensive workouts as well. Both are important and complementary—in the same way that proteins are not better for our body than vitamins.

You must first try to incorporate the six gems I have described in the previous chapter. These are extremely important. In addition to these, try to incorporate the short holistic workouts I've outlined in this chapter.

An intense workout is almost like an assault on the body! After a workout, when you rest and give your body proper nutrition, the body repairs itself. It becomes stronger and better in all the aspects of fitness that your workout involved.

Rest and nutrition are as important as the workout. That is why we will have at least a day's rest between two workouts. On the rest day, some light exercise is fine. It is not fine, however, to keep pushing the same muscles again and again while they are still in recovery mode.

The kind of workout we will be doing actually goes much beyond the physical aspect of our fitness. These workouts are aimed at all-round functional fitness and complete wellness. Even in the short workouts, I have incorporated yoga postures, Suryanamaskars, relaxation techniques, and deep breathing in the warm-ups and cool downs, making them complete mind-and-body workouts. These workouts will not just improve your fitness but enhance your overall health and well-being at the same time.

Each workout has three parts: the warm-up, the main workout, and the cool down. I am outlining what you need to know and keep in mind in preparation for the workout—during the workout and after it.

Preparation

Buy comfortable—preferably cotton—breathable workout clothes from a sports shop.

Buy running shoes that are light and flexible, which are good for both brisk walking and jogging. The soles of the shoes should not be too soft or too hard and the shoes should not be tight. When you are in the shop, wear the shoes and walk around, try jogging or hopping around a bit to check how they feel.

Buy a yoga mat or find a dari suitable for floor exercises, which will give you a slight cushioning when you lie down for the floor exercises.

Keep room temperature water near you. Take small sips when you feel thirsty so you do not get dehydrated when you sweat. If you are doing the whole workout at a park, carry a bottle of water with you.

Make sure the air conditioner and fan remain off during the workout. If it is too hot or stuffy, keep the fan on low. Open the windows to let in some fresh air.

Many people like to play music while they walk or jog. I do not advise playing music while working out. Listening to music takes your attention away from your environment and, worse, your body and technique. When you're warming up outdoors, take time to enjoy the fresh air and, if you're lucky enough, whatever nature or greenery there might be around you.

Warm-Up

The purpose of a warm-up is to prepare your body for the main workout. Apart from ensuring better technique and range of movement through the workout, warming up greatly reduces the chances of injury.

Working out, to draw an analogy, is similar to driving a car in some ways. For instance, to ensure a smooth driving experience, both for the people in the car and for the car itself, it's good to start the engine and let the car heat up for a few seconds. Then you put it in the first gear, then second, third, and fourth, before going at very high speed. I know these days most cars have very fast pick up and are automatic, but I'm a bit old fashioned, just like our bodies!

A warm-up similarly involves first heating up the body and gradually preparing it for the high-intensity movements of the main workout.

Just because the warm-up exercises are easy and a bit repetitive, do not ignore or rush through them, as they are extremely important.

Anita, who has been working out with me for three years now, did not like the part where I made her do a walk outdoors for a warm-up and would ask me, 'Can we skip the walk and start directly with the main workout today?' or 'I already did a walk two hours back so now can we move straight to the main workout?' My answer would always be, 'No'.

It is important to heat up the body before the main workout so no, the warm-up can't be skipped, and no, heating up the body even one hour before is not good enough as the body has already cooled down after the hour is up. The main workout needs to be done right after a warm-up, while you are still sweating and the blood is still circulating fast. Just like if we were to work on moulding iron, it would need to be heated and then moulded immediately, while it is still hot.

I like the idea of warming up outdoors with a nice cardio, like a brisk walk or a jog and then coming indoors for the main workout. Since it is less breezy indoors, your body will stay warmed up longer through your workout which will, in turn, help you exercise more efficiently and also reduce the chances of injury.

To heat up the body, we need to do an activity that raises our heart rate but is not too vigorous. A brisk walk, slow jog, or cycling are all great for warming-up. Once you start to sweat a bit and the heart rate goes up, you can stop and do the warm-up stretches and rotations. How long you need to do the cardio activity to heat up the body depends on the weather. If it's very hot and humid, the body will get heated up quickly, but if it is cold, you might have to warm up for longer. Be careful not to overdo the cardio in the warm-up as you might exhaust all your energy, which you will need for the main workout. Make sure to do the joint rotations and stretches slowly and not rush through them.

In my own workouts, I divide the warm-up into two stages, especially when I am doing something more vigorous in the main workout. For example, if I am including short sprints in my main workout on a particular day, then I might start my warm-up by walking, followed by stretches and rotations, followed by some jogging, and then some more stretches to prepare for the vigorous movement of sprinting.

Main Workout

To work out well is an art. My fitness teacher used to say that a workout should be done with the awareness and precision of a surgeon. Don't push yourself too much or too little, it should be just right. The art is in finding that point which is just right and then in pushing yourself to that point, but not beyond.

Pay extra attention to your technique and form while working out. Get the technique right in the first couple of sessions, and then start pushing yourself in those exercises. If your technique of doing squats is not right just yet, go slow, go easy. If you push too much with the wrong technique, you might injure your knees or back over a period of time. When in doubt, go slow and do less. If you feel pain, just stop.

I know I've stressed this point already, but it is extremely important to remember—there must be at least a day's gap between intense workouts. The body must recuperate. The rest will only make you stronger.

Cool Down

Like the warm-up before the main workout, a cool down after the workout is absolutely essential. After increasing your heart rate and contracting your muscles excessively in the workout, it is important to get your body back to a normal state as you finish your session. The cool down consists of gentle cardio exercises and stretching and rotations similar to the warm-up.

The cool down helps to bring the heart rate back to normal, gets the blood circulation flowing evenly throughout the body, helps the muscles relax, and aids the process of flushing out lactic acid from the muscles, reducing the post workout pain and discomfort. Just like the warm-up, the cool down reduces the chances of injury and is indispensable.

After the workout, if you feel any discomfort, stiffness, or imbalance in any part of the body, you should do specific

stretches and yoga postures to recreate balance and relax those muscles. For example if you have excessively strained your lower back then relax it by getting into Pavanmuktasana (page 60) to relax the lower back.

It is nice to end the cool down with relaxation techniques which further activate the healing and repair of the body.

Post Workout

You can expect to feel fit, energetic, relaxed, and rejuvenated. You might also feel some pain in the muscles. My martial arts teacher used to call this 'sweet pain'. This is the slight pain caused by a build up of lactic acid in your muscles, which is normal when you put your muscles through a series of vigorous contractions. You are more likely to feel this slight pain when you wake up the next morning.

At this point, the muscles need good rest and nutrition to become stronger. If you want, you can do some light exercise or a walk and some stretches that will actually help reduce the 'sweet pain' in the muscles.

This is good pain, but there is also possibility of bad pain. The bad pain, particularly in your lower back, neck, knees, or shoulders, could be because you overdid something or did some movement with a jerk or wrong technique. This kind of pain is not good news. If it persists even after a day of rest, you should skip the next workout or do something gentle which does not involve the affected part. When the pain is greatly reduced and you do resume workouts—in the beginning, go easy on muscle contractions involving that part, and focus more on stretching.

In the event of a sudden injury while working out, stop exercising and put ice on the affected part to arrest swelling.

Though you should take precautions, don't be afraid of pain or injuries. They're a part of any athlete's life, and as long as you deal with them correctly, they will only make your body stronger.

Post workout, the two most important things are rest and diet. Get good sleep. Make sure you eat a nutritious, balanced, and fresh food diet. Apart from other nutrients, try to keep your natural diet rich in protein and drink lots of water.

Your Workout Routine

Time

Each time you do a workout, you'll need to take out around 30 minutes. That's the minimum. If you have the time or feel like doing more, you can always stretch the workout to around 45 minutes by increasing the brisk walking or jogging in your warm-up as well as the duration of relaxation exercises in the cool down. A few weeks into the workout, you can do another set of exercises in the main workout on the days you have more time.

How many times a week do you think you can take out a minimum of 30 minutes? Those 30 minutes can be either in the morning or the evening—whatever suits you. The ideal is three days a week on alternate days. If that's not possible, then two days a week. Or is only one day a week a realistic possibility?

- Three days a week: You'll now need to decide which days you'll schedule your workout. For example, you could schedule your workout on Monday, Wednesday, and Friday evenings after work. Or you could do Sunday morning, and then Tuesday and Friday evenings. However you want to design it, just remember, you'll need to give a day's rest in between the workouts.

- Two days a week: If you feel you can carve out two days a week, try to figure out when that might be. Once over the weekend and once mid-week?
- One day a week: Can you only take out time over the weekend? Or does one day in the week sound more doable?

Find whatever combination suits you best and put it in your calendar as your workout time. Try as much as you can to stick to the days—or day—you've chosen. But don't get too hassled if you miss a workout. Don't worry that you've lost momentum. Schedule it for another day. The only rule is to leave at least a day's gap.

If you choose to do a workout just twice or once a week, try and brisk walk or jog whenever you find the time on the remaining days. Follow the walk or jog with exercises given in the 'Six Gems'. On days where you just find 10 to 15 minutes which are not enough to do a workout, or even an outdoor brisk walk, you can do a short warm-up that we did for the 20-minute routines in Chapter 4 and follow it with selected exercises from 'Six Gems' in Chapter 5.

How the Workouts are Devised

Do make sure you've gone through all of Chapter 4 before you start the workout. In the workout, you will need to follow the same precautions and pay extra attention to your weak points. Additionally, the terms explained at the end of Chapter 2 will help you understand the workout better.

As outlined in the previous section, 'Basics of a Workout', the workouts are divided into three segments: Warm-up, Main workout, and Cool down.

In our workouts, the warm-up is further divided into five steps to be done one after the other—Heating Up the Body 1, Warm-up Exercises 1, Heating Up the Body 2, Warm-up Exercises 2, and some yoga postures and stretches.

The warm-up addresses a key aspect of fitness—your stamina—through the cardio exercises. It also focuses on another aspect of fitness—your flexibility—through the stretches, rotations, and yoga postures.

The main workout focuses more on strength. Since this is an athletic workout, we include strengthening exercises for the whole body in a single session rather than selected muscles. In a gym or other forms of workouts, you might find many people taking a little break between two strength exercises. Here we do a connecting exercise, which helps make optimum use of time, keeps the heart rate up, and increases the overall intensity of the workout session. I have allotted enough time to each exercise so you do not need to rush through them.

Make sure to avoid any jerky movement and maintain your form and technique. In the strength exercises in the main workout, do enough repetitions while maintaining the correct form so that you push your muscles slightly beyond their present capacity. For example, if 7 push-ups are absolutely comfortable for you, try to do 10, pushing the muscles a little beyond their present capacity. As the muscles become stronger in the following weeks, you will be able to do 15 comfortably.

But do not try to push up to 15 at present, if even 10 are quite challenging, as you might injure yourself.

Easy and Advanced Exercise Versions

In the main workout, the exercises have easy and advanced variations. If you are starting workouts for the first time or after a long gap; if you are not familiar with the exercise and not sure about your technique; if you are not so young or not so fit at present—then start with the easy versions of the exercises. You should listen to your body and avoid exercises which are too strenuous for you right now.

If you are fit and the gentle versions don't challenge you at all, then you can do the advanced versions. If you are not too sure then I would advise you to start with the gentle versions, prepare your muscles, and perfect your technique over a few workouts before moving on to the advanced versions.

If you are very fit already and want to make your workouts even more challenging, I will be showing more exercise variations for you in the next chapter.

The cool down is also divided into three parts. Gentle cardio, cool down exercises which mainly involve stretching exercises to relax the muscles, and finally, relaxation which involves relaxing yoga postures and deep breathing.

The whole workout has been devised to make optimum use of time and yet be a complete workout addressing all aspects of fitness and incorporating elements of yoga. The yoga postures are included in the warm-up and cool down in a way that they enhance the whole session without losing the essence of a true workout or true yoga practice.

On the days you are running short of time, cut down on the yoga postures from both the warm-up and cool down, because yoga postures need to be done slowly to absorb their full holistic benefits. Don't ever try and rush through yoga postures. It's a waste of time. If, on the other hand, you have more than 30 minutes for the routine, spend time holding each yoga posture longer. Also increase the warm-up cardio by 5 to 10 minutes on the days you have more time.

As you did in the one-month commitment, you can carry your mat to the park and do the whole routine at the park itself. Alternatively, you can do the 'Heating Up the Body' part of the warm-up outside your house and come back home for warm-up stretches and the remaining workout.

The Basic Workout

Warm-up: 12 minutes

The warm-up for our workout has five stages. The first four stages from, Heating Up the Body 1 to Warm-up Exercises 2, are the same as we did for the 20-minute routine for our one-month commitment and should take you 9 minutes. The fifth part, 'Some Yoga Postures and Stretches', has been described.

Heating Up the Body 1 (page 76)
Warm-up Exercises 1 (page 76 to 78)
Heating Up the Body 2 (page 79)
Warm-up Exercises 2 (page 79 to 86)

Some Yoga Postures and Stretches

Sit on your mat and attempt the following yoga postures as continuation of the warm-up. Do the yoga postures slowly without rushing through them.

Vajrasana (Thunderbolt posture)

Sit in Vajrasana for 15 seconds.

Janushirasana (Forward one leg toe touching) (page 134 to 135)

Hold the stretch for 15 seconds on each leg.

Dynamic Purvottanasana (Dynamic toe touching) Variation 2 (page 136 to 137)

Repeat three times with breathing-movement coordination. Exhale when you bend forward and inhale when you raise your hips up.

Titaliasana (Butterfly stretch) (page 91 to 92)
Hold the stretch for 20 seconds.

3 cycles of Suryanamaskar (page 141 to 145)
You can avoid or go easy on the postures in Suryanamaskar which are too difficult for you.

Main workout: 12 Minutes
Upper body strengthening Set 1:
Push-ups (page 101 to 102)

Easy Version

Push-ups with knee support (page 101)

Push-ups with wall support (page 102)

Alternatively, you can do the advanced version.

Advanced Version

Technique: In the starting position for the advanced version of push-ups, the knees and hips are up. Your body weight is slightly more on your arms than your toes, which are turned inwards. Breathe in as you bend your elbows and lower your body towards the floor while keeping it straight. Lower the body enough to almost touch your chest to the floor but without resting your body on the floor. Now straighten your elbows to come up to the starting position while breathing in. This is one push-up.

Choose the variation of push-ups that is comfortable for you. If push-ups with knee support are also difficult for you, then do the wall support push-ups. Find a short wall or a table or a window ledge roughly your shoulder height to do them.

Do 6 push-ups, or according to your capacity.
Connecting exercise:

Front leg raises

Do this as per your capacity. You don't have to raise the leg too
high if it is challenging. You can take support of a wall with
your hand if balancing is difficult. Do not raise the leg with a
jerk, do it gently.

Repeat three times with each leg.
Upper body strengthening Set 2:

Tricep dips (page 132 to 133)

Easy Version

Alternatively, you can do the advanced version.

Advanced Version

Technique: To do the advanced version of the tricep dips, place the hands on a bench, shoulder-width apart, the way you did for the easier version. Now stretch your feet in front of you, keeping the knees straight so that when you bend your elbows for the dips, they make a ninety-degree angle, working mainly your upper back and triceps muscles.

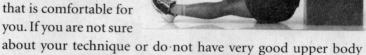

Choose the version that is comfortable for you. If you are not sure about your technique or do not have very good upper body strength yet, then stick to the easier version for now.

Do 6 tricep dips or according to your capacity.

Connecting exercise:

Front and back leg raises

Technique: Taking an external support like a wall with your right hand, stand on your right leg, and gently swing your left leg up in front of you and then take it back behind you in

a continuous movement. Do not try to raise the leg too high beyond your capacity and do not do this with a jerk. After doing this a few times on one leg, turn the other side and repeat the same with the other leg.

Repeat three times with each leg.

Leg strengthening:

Squats (page 69 to 70)
To make the squats more challenging, you can do them more slowly and hold the final position for longer before coming up.

Repeat 6 times or according to your capacity.

Back strengthening:

Easy Version

Back strengthening variation 1 (page 97)

Advanced Version

Back strengthening variation 2 (page 97 to 98)

Repeat the easy version twice and then the advanced version twice. If variation 2 is difficult for you then repeat variation 1 again.

Connecting exercise:

Tiger stretch variation 2 (page 162)

Repeat two times with each leg.

Stomach strengthening Set 1:

Stomach muscles are very resilient and we will be working on them a little extra. In the following exercise we will be working on strengthening our core—the stomach as well as back muscles.

Easy Version

Lying down single leg raise (page 129)

If this exercise is strenuous enough, then continue four times with each leg, else after 2 repetitions, move on to the next, slightly advanced exercise—Dynamic toe touching Variation 1—an excellent and important exercise.

Advanced Version

Dynamic toe touching variation 1 (page 98 to 99)
    Repeat three times.

Dynamic toe touching variation 1 challenging version 1 (page 159)

To make the previous exercise more challenging, you could raise your knees as you come up. If this is too strenuous at present then avoid this and do the previous easier version instead.

Repeat three times.

Connecting exercise:

Side leg raises

Technique: Lie down sideways with your legs together, your head supported with your hand with the elbow bent and resting on the floor. Put the other hand in front of you near your stomach to help you balance. Gently and slowly, raise up the leg which is on top as high as comfortably possible with your knees straight and the toes turned outwards, pointing towards your head. Immediately after raising the leg, bring it down slowly back to the starting position. After completing the counts with one

leg, turn to the other side and repeat equal number of times with the other leg.

Repeat three times with one leg and then turn the other side to repeat with the other.

Stomach strengthening Set 2:

Easy Version

Lying down cycling movement

Technique: Lie down on your back with your hands along the sides of your body and palms facing down. Bend both the knees and raise the legs up. Now start a cycling motion with your legs. Stretch each leg completely while bending the other one. The movement should be circular and gentle, roughly at a sixty-degree angle to the floor. For the first few cycles, the movement of the stretched leg should be up downwards. For the next few cycles bring the stretched leg from down upwards in a reverse cycling movement.

Repeat three times in the forward cycling movement and three times in a reverse cycling movement.

Alternatively, you can do this advanced exercise.

Advanced Version

Hands behind the neck leg raises
(page 163 to 164)

Repeat three or four times.

Follow the previous stomach exercise, easy or advanced, and follow it up with crunches to further intensify stomach contractions in this final set for stomach muscles.

Crunches (page 165)

Do about 10 crunches or according to your capacity.

Cool down: 6 Minutes

Gentle cardio

Walk at a gentle pace for 1 minute.

Cool down exercises

Do the cool down stretches at a gentle pace.
Standing toe touching (page 77)

Do this three times.

Side stretch (page 79 to 80)

Once on each side. Hold the stretch
for 10 seconds on each.

Forward and backward bend (page 80 to 81)
Repeat two times. Hold the stretch for 10
seconds each time.

Shoulder rotation (page 83)
Two times clockwise and two times anticlockwise.

Hip rotation (page 85)

Rotate the hips in a circular
movement, two times clockwise
and two times anticlockwise.

Knee stretch 1 (page 77)

Knee stretch 2 (page 85)

Do the 'Knee stretch 1' on each leg once,
holding the stretch for 4 seconds each

time. Similarly, do the 'Knee stretch
2' on each leg, holding the stretch
for 4 seconds each time. If you find
it difficult to balance, then you
could do this taking wall support
with one hand.

Relaxation
Shavasana (page 58 to 59)

Relax in Shavasana for 1 minute. After 30 seconds you can put your hands on your stomach to be more aware of your breathing.

Deep breathing (page 203 to 204)
Sit still in a comfortable position for 30 seconds and then take three deep breaths.

Do the 'Basic Workout' for at least one to two weeks.

In the next chapter, 'Vary Your Routine', I'll take you through different variations you can incorporate within the basic workout you've just completed.

Exactly when you want to vary your workout depends on you. It depends on how many times a week you're managing to exercise. Always listen to your body.

When you get comfortable with the 'Basic Workout', I'd like you to think about why you are working out. Start to think about some goals you'd like to conquer. We'll be discussing some possible goals in the next section, after which we'll move on to varying and intensifying your workout.

Set Your Own Goals

So you've practised the one-month commitment and learnt the 'Six Gems'. You've figured out your strengths and weaknesses. And now you've started a workout regimen marking your calendar. You have reached a wonderful milestone.

It is time now to set some goals. Setting these goals will give you direction in your workouts and keep you motivated.

Appearance Goals

For most people their fitness goals are centred on how their body looks now and how they want it to look once they put in all the effort. This is okay to start with, but I would advise you to focus more on your fitness goals as once you become truly fit, your body will automatically be at its most attractive.

A healthy glow

Every one of us wants to have a 'healthy glow' on our face, which is actually a result of many factors which affect our health and state of well-being. It is a reflection of a healthy diet, right exercise, adequate sleep, and a calm mind, among other factors.

To increase the glow on your face, you should make sure to include deep breathing exercises, relaxation techniques like Shavasana, back-bending postures like the cobra to improve the condition of your spine, postures that improve blood circulation to your face like the rabbit posture and cardio exercises like jogging, cycling, or brisk walking, which increase blood circulation and make you sweat in your routine.

Sit still for a few minutes every day, practise static yoga postures and dynamic techniques like the Suryanamaskar which improve the flow of pranic energy in the body, improving your aura, which reflects on your face.

Losing weight

To achieve this goal, you'll have to particularly focus on the cardio aspect of your workout. If you want to lose weight, try to increase the time and intensity of the cardio, in both the warm-up and cool down.

In the warm-up, increase the time of the cardio exercise by few minutes. You should also try to increase the intensity.

In the cool down, you can add in some low-intensity cardio, like a walk, slow spot jogging, or stair climbing.

Apart from your workout, include brisk walking, jogging, and stair climbing as much as you can on a daily basis, along with restricting your calorie intake to reach your goal quickly.

Gaining weight

If you want to increase your weight, then do not overdo the cardio exercise and focus more on the strength exercises and yoga postures. Most importantly, eat a diet rich in healthy carbohydrates, proteins, and fat. Just because you need to gain weight does not mean you should eat junk or fried food. That only serves to harm your health. Include bananas, full cream milk, ghee, nuts, potatoes, and rice in your diet. Increase the portions of the home-cooked healthy food to make sure your calorie intake increases to more than what you are currently consuming.

Do not make wanting to gain weight a reason for you to not work out. Focus more on strength training exercises like push-ups and squats in your workouts and eat a protein-rich diet. This will help you build muscle when you rest your muscles adequately after the workout.

Lean yet muscular

To be lean, focus on both your cardio and flexibility through brisk walking, jogging, and the practice of yoga postures and stretches. To be muscular, pay extra attention to the freehand strength training exercises like push-ups, squats, dips, pull-ups, and stomach- and back-strengthening exercises in the main workout. A combination of both kinds of exercise will keep you lean yet muscular.

In the main workout, try to do two to three sets of the freehand strength-training exercises. Once you finish one round of the main workout, start another round. This time, work your muscles to the maximum of their capacity and then try to go a little beyond. For example, in the second round of push-ups, after you do as many as you can comfortably, try to do a few more, pushing the muscles a little beyond their present capacity. Try to maintain the proper technique and not do any movement with a jerk, even when you're pushing yourself. Go easy for the first three weeks of the workout before you start pushing yourself using this method of training.

In addition to the strength exercises using your own body weight, like push-ups, you could also introduce exercises with dumb-bells in your workout. (page 288 to 293)

Give your muscles adequate rest after the workout and increase the protein intake in your diet. Increase intake of milk, eggs, daal, chicken, fish, sprouts, and almonds.

Fitness Goals

Conquering weaknesses

We all have our own strengths and weaknesses. The first step is to recognize them by practising various yoga postures and other exercises like we did in the previous chapters. You might discover that you have good overall strength but low flexibility or vice versa. You might even be strong or flexible in certain parts of the body and weak or stiff in others.

Muscle contraction exercises like push-ups and squats improve strength; stretching exercises including many yoga postures improve flexibility; deep breathing exercises calm the mind; and cardiovascular exercises like brisk walking, jogging, and cycling improve stamina.

Whatever your weaknesses—stiff upper back, weak arms, low stamina, bad posture, shallow breathing, or a very restless mind—pay extra attention to them in your workouts to conquer them over a period of time. By doing that you will move towards your optimum all round fitness and consequently feel, look, and be truly fit.

Master more challenging yoga postures

First master the basic yoga postures and the Suryanamaskar that I have described in the 'Six Gems'. Even the other easier postures like Bhujangasana(Cobra posture) and Vrikshasana(Tree posture) that I have mentioned earlier need a lot of practice to master. Just doing something that looks like Bhujangasana is not enough. We must strive towards perfection and grace in each posture and then increase the duration that we can hold each posture. With practice, over a period of time, you should be able to hold the static postures for over a minute.

Once you have perfected the simpler postures, you could work towards other more challenging ones and try to perfect them gradually. I have not given the steps nor explained the technique of the postures shown; the challenging postures should only be attempted and learnt under the guidance of an expert.

Padmasana

Utthita Padmasana

Poorna Naukasana

Supta Virasana

Sarvangasana

Halasana

Natarajasana

Parsvakonasana

Ek Padasana

Bakasana

Chakrasana

Shirshasana

Master advanced freehand exercises

In the earlier chapters, you have practised some important freehand exercises. I hope you have perfected the technique of those exercises and are able to comfortably do a few repetitions of each exercise.

I am listing some more freehand exercises which are more challenging. You could gradually work towards perfecting these according to your capacity. Some of these, like skipping, short sprints, and pull-ups might be too high intensity for many people and will be more suited to people who are quite fit already. High-intensity exercises like skipping give good results with minimal time investment. However, you have to work gradually towards getting perfection in their technique first, else you could injure yourself.

You can make it your goal to do an advanced version of push-ups (page 227) or a challenging stomach exercise like 'hands behind the neck leg raise' (page 163 to 164) with ease. Practising the easier versions of the upper body and stomach exercises for now will enable you for the more challenging versions once you have strengthened your muscles.

Similarly, to achieve perfection in skipping which is an excellent exercise—you will first need to strengthen and condition your leg muscles through light jogging and squats over a few weeks and then start working towards perfecting skipping.

If you are unsure about your technique, you should seek expert guidance to help you learn these and other challenging exercises. Also, remember to warm up well before practising high-intensity movements like skipping or sprinting.

We will be using some of the exercises I have mentioned here to vary our workouts. I will explain that in the next chapter.

Push-ups, advanced version with legs at a height

Technique: The technique of these push-ups is similar to the advanced version of the push-ups (page 227). The only difference is that in these, your legs are at a height above the floor while your hands are on the floor. In this position, more of your body weight shifts to your arms, making these push-ups more challenging. The higher you put your legs the more challenging it will be for you.

Dand push-up variation (Easy and advanced versions)

Traditional Indian wrestlers practise this dynamic push-up. This is also a part of the Suryanamaskar. Perfecting these will improve this movement in your Suryanamaskar practice as well.

Technique: For the easier version, start with knees rested on the ground. For the more challenging version, keep your knees up. While breathing in, lower your body by bending the elbows backwards, keeping them close to the body. In a continuous movement, take your head and upper body forward and then up, creating an upward arc to come into the cobra position. This is one dand. Now raise your hips up and go back to the starting position for the next. Breathe out while going back to the starting position.

For the next cycle, put the knees down if you are doing the easier version. For the advanced version, lower your body keeping the shoulders, hips, and the knees in the same line without resting your body weight on the knees. In this more challenging version, after lowering the body close to the floor, start arching up using your arm strength without resting your body weight on the floor completely.

Dynamic toe touching variation 1— challenging version 2

Technique: This is similar to 'Dynamic toe touching variation 1—challenging version 1' (page 159). When you come up from the lying-down position, raise the legs up keeping the knees straight to come up in a full Naukasana position(page 68). Hold that position for a fraction of a second before going back to the lying down position for the next cycle.

Do not attempt this if the earlier, less challenging versions are not yet comfortable for you.

Sideways lunges (Easy and advanced variations)

Easy Version

Technique: Stand with the distance between your feet about double your shoulder width. Raise both hands in front, parallel to the floor for balance and bend your right knee, shifting your body weight more to your right leg. Your knee should be bent at about a ninety-degree angle. Now come back to the starting position with your weight equally on both legs and then bend the left knee and shift your weight on it. This should be done while you are facing the front.

Advanced Version
Technique: In the advanced version, after bending the right knee go all the way down, bending the knee completely. In the final position, the hips are close to the floor, the right leg flat on the ground and your left leg stretched straight. Your body weight is almost entirely on your right leg and you are resting on the heel of the left leg with the left toes pointing up. Now come up from this position slowly,

straightening your right leg. Repeat the same on the left side with the left leg.

Round kick
Technique: Stand with your feet a little more than

shoulder-width apart, your hands to the sides and a little away from the body for balance. Raise the right leg and take it to your left side, crossing over in front of the left leg and then up, creating a circular movement to come back to the starting position. Repeat the same on the other side with your left leg.

Shadow boxing: Punches with footwork

Earlier, we had practised some straight punches from a stationary position. In shadow boxing, you move as you throw the punches as if you are fighting an imaginary opponent.

To perfect the footwork and punching coordination you require a lot of practice but once you master it, it is a great and fun exercise.

Technique: The punches are the straight punches that we attempted earlier (page 156 to 157). For the footwork—if you are standing with your right foot forward, while throwing the right punch take your right leg six inches forward. Follow it up by immediately throwing a punch with your left hand and simultaneously moving your left leg six inches forward. Now as you step back, throw the right punch while you take your left leg six inches back. Follow it by throwing the left punch while moving the right leg back six inches. Remember, moving forward— same leg, same hand. Moving backwards—opposite hand, opposite leg. You can even hold your punches and just move forward and back using this footwork and then resume the punches. To get a better idea of footwork, the boxing movies I

recommended earlier for straight punches (page 156 to 157) will help!

Jumping Jacks

Technique: Stand with your feet together and hands by your side, palms open and facing inward. With a smooth jump get into the second position where your feet are more than your shoulder-width apart and your hands are a little above shoulder height, completely stretched out. (This position, incidentally, is

much like the figure in the famous Leonardo da Vinci's painting, *Vitruvian Man*!) Now immediately jump back to get into the starting position. Do this as a continuous movement, jumping from the first position into the second position. Be light on your feet. Breathe in when your stretch your arms and feet, breathe out when you join your feet together.

Skipping

Technique: You can use a skipping rope if you are practising this outdoors or where you have enough space around you. Otherwise, just imagine a rope in your hands. Jump on your toes while simultaneously rotating your wrists like you would to turn the rope. Land very lightly on your toes. Don't jump too high, just enough to allow the rope to pass beneath your feet. Do not land with a thumping sound as that would jar your joints. It takes practice to perfect effortless, light-on-your-feet skipping.

You could initially practise skipping without a rope on a soft surface like grass or mud as that would be gentler on your joints till you find the right technique.

Short sprints

Technique: In the picture, I have shown an 'on your marks' position, which you would take to start a sprint. You do not

necessarily need to start in that position. Short sprints could be anything from 20 to 50 metres. Run this distance with big, powerful strides. Warm up well by jogging and doing some stretches. Land on your toes while sprinting. You could do these three times with up to a minute's rest in between. You could sprint one way and then walk back to the starting point to run again.

Pull-ups variation 1(Easy and advanced versions)

Easy Version

Technique: If the bar is at a height, stand on a stool and hold the bar with both hands, with your palms facing inwards towards your face. Hands should be shoulder-width apart. In the starting position, your hands, shoulders, and the

bar should be at the same level with your elbows completely bent, as if you have pulled yourself using your hands though your feet are on the stool. In this easy version you do not hang onto the bar completely, keeping most part of your body weight on your feet which are comfortably planted on the stool. Now lower your body partly using your arm strength and partly using the leg muscles as you bend your knees simultaneously. Come down to the point where your elbows are at a ninety-degree angle. Pull yourself up to the starting position again using your arm strength as well as your legs.

In this easy version of pull-ups, you decide how much body weight you want to shift on your arms and how much to keep on your legs.

Advanced Version

In the advanced version, you do not stand on a stool and you do not distribute your body weight between your arms and your legs. You take it completely on your arms and upper body.

Stand by hanging completely on the bar with hands shoulder-width apart and palms facing inward. Raise your body using your upper-body strength to the point where your elbows are completely bent and your shoulders are in line with the bar. Now lower the body to the point where your elbows are at a ninety-degree angle. Now again come up for the next pull–up. Do as many as you comfortably can.

Warm up well by heating up the body with a cardio exercise and stretches including shoulder rotations before you do these.

Pull-ups variation 2 (Easy and advanced versions)

Technique: The pull-up variation 2, easy and advanced versions, is very similar to the pull-up variation 1 (page 262 to 263). The only difference is in the way you grip the bar. In this version, hold the bar with your hands a little wider than shoulder-width apart and your palms facing outward, away from your face.

Advanced Tricep dips with raised legs

Technique: The technique is similar to the advanced version of the tricep dips (page 132 to 133). In this case, your legs need to be at the same height at which you have your hand grip. This way, when you lower your body, your hands are bearing more of your body weight than in the earlier version. For this, you can use two bars at the same height or place two tables of similar height to rest your hands and legs.

Hanging leg raises for abs

Technique: Hang onto a bar with your hands shoulder-width apart. Raise both the knees up slowly till the knees are bent at a ninety-degree angle. Hold that position for a few seconds and then bring the knees down to come back to the starting

position. Repeat this a few times. It will be easier for you if you have a back support while you do this.

Make functional fitness goals

This to me is the most exciting part of working out. What are you regularly working out for? At least once in a while, you should do some activity that tests your fitness in several ways. In a workout, everything is too controlled and predictable. Once you have become reasonably fit, it is time to push boundaries and test your functional fitness. Playing a sport or going for a long run or a trek are good ways to do that. Make your own functional fitness goals and let your workouts prepare you for that.

I have been training a group of reasonably fit people, mostly in their late twenties and thirties. We do a regular workout, similar to what I have outlined for you in the earlier section, on Tuesday and Thursday mornings. On Saturday mornings, we do an activity where we get to push the limits of our functional fitness. Often we do a 3-km run on a hilly terrain followed by a game of basketball or badminton. Occasionally, we've gone cycling or some days we run on the beach followed by a game of football. At least once a month we do a 6 to 7 km run. The ones who can't run all the way run a bit then walk. There have been people who couldn't even do half the longer run when they started and are now able to run all the way with relative ease. Over time, they've increased their stamina and become much fitter. Once, I took the group for wall climbing, which turned out to be a great activity to test and enhance their functional fitness. Even if they are travelling, they are inspired to keep up their exercise on their own and stay on par with the others to avoid struggling when we do these challenging activities.

You have to find your own functional fitness goal which inspires you to keep up your fitness level and be regular with your workouts. I can give you a few ideas.

- A game of badminton, football, or any other sport every week or fortnight
- Climbing seven flights of steps effortlessly
- Going for a trek or other adventure sports which require you to be fit
- Brisk walking or jogging 5 or 10 km within a certain time you set for yourself
- Playing outdoors with children and matching their energy and fitness
- Being able to push your car or change a tyre if you need to
- To run the next marathon
- Being able to walk or jog effortlessly to your friend's house who lives close by
- When you travel, having the basic fitness to walk or climb while exploring new places

The list can be endless. Your functional fitness goal can be ambitious or modest, but it should inspire you to keep up regular exercise.

Vary Your Routine

So now you've set some goals for yourself. Once you have gotten into a flow and grasped the basics of your workout—you can start to vary your workout. When that is, is entirely up to you. It could be after a week or two weeks. You should be the judge of that. The timelines I have given in this section are only indicative.

While the basic structure of the workout remains the same—warm-up, main workout, cool down—you can start to think about varying your workouts in two different ways. You can vary the intensity of your workout as well as the exercises in the basic workout.

Varying the Intensity

Varying the intensity in the first month of starting a workout

Week One

This is the first week of getting to know the basics of the workout. Let the muscles get used to the exercises. Focus on perfecting the technique rather than doing too many repetitions in the strength training exercises like push-ups and squats. Try to learn the technique of jogging better and strive to get a rhythm when you're jogging rather than pushing yourself too hard or too long. Don't push yourself for the first week. Learn all the exercises and practise them well within your comfort level.

Week Two

In the second week, you can begin to push yourself slightly. In each exercise, try to push yourself close to your maximum capacity. For example, if you can do 10 push-ups comfortably, with good technique, then go up to 10 and stop.

Week Three

In the third week, push yourself a little beyond your comfort zone. Towards the end of the cardio in the warm-up, push the intensity of your brisk walk or jog a little more. If you can do 10 push-ups comfortably, push yourself slightly to do 12 or 14.

Week Four

In the fourth week, go a little easier again. Let the intensity be similar to that of Week Two.

As I've said before, working out is an art. It is not just a linear progression in which you can keep increasing the intensity every day, every week, every month till you are doing 500 push-ups and running 500 km!

Vary the intensity of your workouts creatively. Create cycles in your workout routine every day, every week, every month and every few months according to your evolving goals.

You've heard about sportspeople and athletes planning their year, choosing some tournaments, and missing others. Their workouts are meticulously designed for the whole year. Also, many a time they might miss a tournament happening at the beginning of a month to perform better at another bigger tournament at the end of the same month. Rest and varying the intensity is a very important consideration for them, as it should be for us.

My martial arts teacher used to make us train very hard, both in terms of fitness and technique, when we were preparing for a competition. Around three days before the actual competition, he'd always tell us to go very easy in order to conserve energy.

Training excessively without giving adequate rest intervals to the body leads to a burnout. It brings down energy levels, immunity, and makes you susceptible to injuries.

So plan your workouts wisely every day over a period of time to avoid burning out.

In case you are not being very regular with your workouts and there has been a gap of three to four days or more, you need to restart at a slightly gentler pace. There will be times when you will miss your workouts. That's all right. Just remember that whenever you are starting after a gap, don't push yourself too hard, and stay well within your comfortable capacity.

If you are regular, the body will get into a flow after two to three weeks of consecutive workouts. Then you can push the body a little harder and increase the intensity progressively, while still creating the cycles that I mentioned earlier.

Varying the intensity within a workout

In Chapter 6, I've explained the basics of each part of our workout in detail for the warm-up, main workout, and cool down. One of the reasons I've done this is so that you can be more creative within your workouts, creating variations based on the structure I have given you.

You can vary your workout depending on how you are feeling on that particular day, what kind of day you're about to have, what kind of weather it is, or simply to make your workout more dynamic.

How are you feeling today?

If you are just feeling plain lazy, then, of course you should find the inner strength to push your body to get it moving. On the other hand, if your body is genuinely feeling weak then you must go easy. Try not to abandon the workout completely. Instead, do an easy walk followed by some gentle yoga postures and deep breathing. This should make you feel much better by boosting your immunity.

On some days if your muscles are in pain, your spine is in discomfort, or your body is still recuperating from your last workout—go easy. Just do some light cardio exercise and focus more on stretches, which will help your muscles relax.

If you feel well rested and full of energy, it is a good day to push your limits in the workout.

What kind of day do you have ahead of you?

If you have a physically strenuous day ahead, don't dissipate too much energy in your workout. Some days when I train Deepika in the morning and she has to shoot a strenuous dance sequence or rehearse for one later that day, we do a lower-intensity workout that involves more stretching. That helps her to perform better yet have energy for her subsequent performance.

What's the weather like?

Hot and humid weather is conducive to good stretching to improve your flexibility.

Winter mornings are great to go for long runs or cycling as you are less likely to get dehydrated or get a sun stroke. Mumbai has long and heavy monsoons. I make it a point to use the outdoors extensively in the remaining months and use the humidity during monsoons for stretching exercises while working out indoors. I must admit that I have taken my students for runs in the rain as well and it is great fun, but only once in a while.

How can I make my workout more dynamic?

You can divide the warm-up and main workout into segments with varying degrees of intensity. Let me give you some examples.

a) Divide up the warm-up: For the initial warm-up, you can do a brisk walk followed by some stretches. After the initial stretches, start jogging for a few minutes, then stop and do more stretches to loosen and warm up the muscles some more. Once the body is well warmed up, you can do an uphill climb, or run up a few flights of stairs, or do short sprints at high intensity.

b) Go for a long brisk walk or jog: Once in a while when the weather is good outside, you can even do a 20-minute jog or brisk walk, and then do the cool-down stretches right after, skipping the main workout section altogether.

c) Do three sets of strengthening exercises: Within the main workout, you can, and should, vary the intensity of different sets of the same exercise. If on a particular day you are focusing more on the strength exercises—do the first set of push-ups, squats, back and stomach strengthening exercises gently. This will prepare those muscles for the next set. In the next set, push the intensity of each of these exercises a little beyond their present capacity. If you are doing 3 sets on a particular day, then you can do the first set easy, push a bit in the second set, and even more in the third set. Alternatively, you can go gentle in the first set, push a lot in the second set, and then go gentler in the third set, which will act like a cool down for the muscles. On the days you push yourself too much with the strength exercises, make sure you cool down properly and include stretches for the muscles you pushed in the main workout. Of course, on the days that you do this, you will have to increase the duration of your workouts accordingly.

Varying the Intensity Over a Week

You should vary the intensity of your workout over a week, going lighter on some days and pushing much harder on other days. Here is a suggested variation for a three-days-a-week workout regime:

a) Workout Day One: Push yourself in the cardio exercises. You can go lighter on the strength exercises today.

b) Workout Day Two: Make your cardio segment shorter today and save energy for more intensive strength training.

c) Workout Day Three: Warm up your body well with the cardio exercises. Skip the strength training today. Since your body is warm, you can do extensive stretching exercises, yoga postures, and deep breathing today.

Of course, your plan for the week would very much depend on which days and how many days in a week you are planning to workout. If I've had a gap of three to four days since my last workout, I generally try to take it easy on my first day back. Similarly, if I know I'm going to have two to three days of rest ahead of me, I push the body a little more.

Keep in mind that you should be reasonably well rested before a high-intensity workout day, and you should keep at least a day's rest after a high-intensity workout. It is a really bad idea to do a high-intensity workout in the evening and follow it up with another high-intensity workout the next morning, unless you are addressing a completely different aspect of fitness the next morning. If, for example, you mainly did excessive push-ups in the evening and went for a longer run the next morning, it's not so bad since you are using a different muscle group and addressing a different aspect of fitness. But I would still not recommend this kind of back-to-back workout because the muscles will still be in recovery mode.

Varying the Intensity Over a Month or More

Just as we do over a week, it is important to vary the intensity of our workouts over a month, three months, or more. The graph of how you plan this is what makes a difference between an ordinary, mechanical workout and an artistic workout. This is important for you whether you are trying to improve your fitness to reach a certain goal or you want to maintain your present fitness.

Your fitness goals will greatly help you decide the intensity variations. Let's say you are planning to train for a 21-km half marathon but can only comfortably run 2 km right now. Say you have nine months to train for it, an the time you can devote for training is around half an hour on Tuesdays and Thursdays, and around one to two hours over the weekend. In this scenario, your rough workout plan towards achieving this goal could look like this:

Marathon Prep: Month One

Increase the duration of the cardio in your Tuesday and Thursday workouts. Start by brisk walking and stretching. Then jog for at least 10 to 15 minutes continuously. To accommodate a longer duration of cardio exercise, you might have to increase the duration of your workout slightly. Or else cut short the main workout by doing just one set of strength exercises before moving on to cool down stretches.

You'll need to do a long run every weekend, progressively increasing and decreasing the duration of the run in cycles over the nine months.

Warm up well before you run. After you finish, stretch the calves and hamstrings well.

Weekend One:	Run 3 km
Weekend Two:	Run 3 km again
Weekend Three:	Stretch it to 4 km
Weekend Four:	Do 3 km again

Marathon Prep: Month Two

In the second month, try to increase the cardio on Tuesdays and Thursdays to 15 or 20 minutes. Make sure to cool down properly.

Weekend One:	Run 4 km
Weekend Two:	Run 4 km again
Weekend Three:	Stretch it to 6 km
Weekend Four:	Do 4 km again

Marathon Prep: Month Three

Keep the 20-minute run on Tuesdays and Thursdays a constant from now until the end of the nine months. Try to increase this duration to 30 to 45 minutes whenever you can.

Weekend One:	Run 4 km
Weekend Two:	Stretch it to 5 km
Weekend Three:	Stretch it further to 7 km
Weekend Four:	Come back to 4 km

Marathon Prep: Month Four

Weekend One:	Start at 5 km
Weekend Two:	Then increase to 7 km
Weekend Three:	Stretch yourself to 10 km
Weekend Four:	Come back to 4 km

Marathon Prep: Month Five

Weekend One:	Start at 6 km
Weekend Two:	Just increase it to 7 km
Weekend Three:	Stretch yourself to 12 km
Weekend Four:	Come back to 5 km

Marathon Prep: Month Six

Weekend One:	Start at 7 km
Weekend Two:	Take it up to 9 km
Weekend Three:	Stretch yourself to 15 km
Weekend Four:	Bring it back down to 5 km

Marathon Prep: Month Seven

Weekend One:	Start the month at 7 km
Weekend Two:	Increase it to 12 km
Weekend Three:	Really stretch yourself to 18 km
Weekend Four:	Bring it back down to 5 km

Marathon Prep: Month Eight

Weekend One:	Start the month at 10 km
Weekend Two:	Bring it back down to 7 km
Weekend Three:	Run 21 km!
Weekend Four:	Ease off to 5 km

Marathon Prep: Month Nine

Weekend One:	Start again at 10 km
Weekend Two:	Overstretch yourself and run 25 km!
Weekend Three:	Bring it back to 7 km
Weekend Four:	End your training at 10 km

Now, assuming the marathon is on the next weekend, you are ready to compete in the marathon rather than just somehow being able to finish it. You'll be able to achieve a decent timing, according to your capacity, and will actually enjoy the experience.

For the week before the marathon, you can do light brisk walks and jogging followed by stretches, but do not do any long run or a strenuous workout. Let your muscles get rest and conserve energy for the main marathon day.

For a month after the marathon, go easier on your weekend runs. On the weekend after the marathon, just rest. The following two weekends, just run up to 5 km.

Marathon Month: Month Ten

Weekend One:	Run the marathon!
Weekend Two:	Rest
Weekend Three:	Just run up to 5 km
Weekend Four:	Again, just 5 km

Now it's time to make a new plan for the next few months with perhaps a new goal!

Even if you are not preparing for the marathon or any other such ambitious goal and want to simply maintain your current level of fitness, you still need to vary your workout intensity. Aside from preventing you from getting bored, you'll get the maximum benefit from your workout by incorporating intensity variation.

Exercise Variations

Apart from varying the intensity, it is also important to vary the exercises within each part of the workout. This breaks monotony and gives the body a more complete workout.

Moreover, since we are striving for true functional fitness, it becomes even more important to introduce such variations in our workout. Every exercise variation uses the muscles in a slightly different way. The more variations there are, the better prepared our muscles will be for any functional situation.

Though we might keep jogging or brisk walking as the main cardio activity for our warm-up, it is good to include side stepping, backward running, stair climbing, and walking or running on different terrains and inclines as variations once in a while.

We might do push-ups as the main upper-body strength exercise, but we should include different variations of push-ups to give the upper body a complete workout and prepare it for different activities. Apart from push–ups, it will be great to do pull-ups occasionally to challenge the muscles of the upper body in a different way. Moreover, just push-ups won't prepare you well for an activity such as rope climbing or wall climbing.

I have listed some exercise variations for your workout. As you start the basic workout, after a few weeks you can take help from this section to include variations of exercises. These exercises will help you enrich your workouts with some diversity while keeping the basic flow the same. For example, for stomach-strengthening exercises in the main workout, you could use the exercises given in the basic workout for the first set, and the variation given here for the second set.

If you get a chance to attend a holistic fitness workshop, you can incorporate more exercises that you learn as variations in your workout.

The exercises in the basic workout that I mentioned earlier and their sequence is the backbone of your workout. Use the exercise variation as an occasional addition or include it in the second set.

Exercise Variations for 'The Basic Workout'

Warm-up

Heating Up the Body 1

279

Spot jogging

Instead of brisk walking, you can do spot jogging for this part of the warm-up. It might be particularly useful when you need to workout in a limited space or don't have time to go out for a walk.

Technique: Run lightly while standing on one spot. Land on your toes. Your arm movement should be similar to when you jog outdoors. Do this barefoot if you are doing it on your mat, otherwise wear shoes if you are doing it on the floor.

Shadow boxing (page 258 to 260)

For this part of the warm-up, keep your movements in shadow boxing slow and gentle as your body is not fully warmed up yet.

Side stepping

Technique: Stand with your feet shoulder-width apart. You will be moving sideways from this position. To go to your right side, take your right leg a few inches further to the right increasing the distance between your feet. Now get your left leg a few inches closer so you are again in a similar position as you started, with shoulder-width distance between your feet. Now again move your right foot and let the left leg follow. Do this 3 to 4 times moving to your right and then similarly move to your left 3 to 4 times leading from your left foot.

Stair climbing

Climb 2 to 3 flights of steps at an easy pace.

Step-ups

Technique: You need just a single step to do this. Stand facing a step. Put the left foot on the step first and then put your right foot beside it. As soon as you put up the right foot, bring the left foot down to its starting position followed by the right foot. Do this eight to ten times, leading from the

left foot to step up and leading from the left itself to step down, with the right foot following after. Now do the same eight to ten times again but this time lead from your right foot and let the left one follow. Do this at a comfortable pace. It should be a slight hopping movement. Be light on your feet.

Warm-up Exercises 1

Tadasana variation 1 (page 122)

Tadasana variation 2 (page 123)

Standing-shoulder and neck back stretch (page 63 to 64)

Heating Up the Body 2

Skipping (page 261)

On-the-spot running
Technique: This is similar to spot jogging (page 280). Only difference is that you need to jog at a faster pace and raise your knees a little higher which makes it a higher-intensity cardio exercise.

Jumping Jacks (page 260 to 261)

Forward and backward running
Technique: Very lightly and taking short steps, run a few steps in the forward direction then run a few steps in the backward direction to come back to where you started. Run on your toes. You can do this barefoot or with shoes on. Be careful while running backward and do it slowly.

Shadow boxing
In this part of the warm-up, you can do the shadow boxing movement a bit faster while maintaining the right technique.

Side stepping
In the earlier part of warm-up, the side-stepping movements were meant to be slow. This time do them faster, more like a shuffling movement.

Short sprints (page 261 to 262)

Warm-up Exercises 2
You can add exercises from the ones given below to the earlier basic warm-up sequence.

Forward lunges

Technique: Take a big step with your right foot and lunge forward bending the right knee to a ninety-degree angle. The right foot should be fully planted on the ground and you are on the toes of your left foot. Both the feet and your body should be pointing in the direction of your forward knee. Interlock your fingers and put your hands, palm facing down, on your right leg just above your knee for balance. Hold that position for a few seconds and come back up slowly. Repeat the same with your left leg forward.

Sideways lunges (Easy and advanced versions) (page 256 to 257)

Full arm rotations

Technique: Stand with the feet a comfortable distance apart. Keep your right hand by your right side and move the left hand in a slow circular movement, clockwise a few times and then anticlockwise the same number of times. Next, keep the left hand stationary and repeat the same with your right hand.

Round kick (page 257 to 258)

Some Yoga Postures and Stretches

Apart from the few yoga postures I have listed in the 'Basic Workout' (page 222 to 242), you could include these along with the other postures that we practised in Chapter 4 for variation.

Vrikshasana (Tree posture) (page 87)

Virbhadrasana (Warrior posture) (page 154 to 155)

Ustrasana (Camel posture) (page 147 to 148)

Bhujangasana (Cobra posture) (page 61 to 62)

Sideways single leg toe touching (page 146)

Both legs forward toe touching (page 125 to 126)

Ardha Naukasana (Half boat posture) (page 93)

Poorna Naukasana (Full boat posture) (page 68)

Utkatasana variation 2 (page 87 to 88)

Main Workout

Upper body strengthening,
Set 1:

Elbow-back push-up

Easy Version

Technique: The technique of these push-ups is similar to push-ups with knee support (page 101). The only difference is that when you lower your body, you bend your elbows inward, keeping it close to your body instead of moving the elbows outward as we did for the earlier push-ups. This variation uses the muscles of the arms a bit differently and is a nice variation to the usual push-up.

Elbow-back push-up

Advanced Version 1

Technique: The technique of this advanced version is similar to the easy version as far as the elbow movement is concerned. The difference is that you keep your knees up in the starting position and not supported on the ground. As you lower your

body, you are taking more weight on your arms without the knee support, making these more challenging.

Elbow-back push up

A more challenging version with legs up

Technique: These are similar to the advanced version 1. Here you put your legs up at a slight height to shift

287

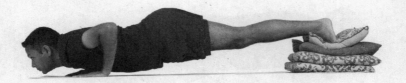

more body weight on your arms, making it even more challenging.

Connecting exercise:
Front kick (page 155 to 156)

Upper body strengthening, Set 2:

Strength training with dumb-bells

Along with strength training using your body weight, it is good to do some strength training with dumb-bells as a variation. These standing exercises with weights are particularly good for functional fitness as they also work on your core muscles, which stabilize the body while you target specific muscles. Do not use very heavy dumb-bells. It should be a comfortable weight allowing you to do around 10 standing bicep curls easily. Follow proper technique and do not do the movement with a jerk as that may cause you injury. Repeat the exercise around ten times in each set and stop when you feel a good contraction in the targetted muscles. In all the following four exercises, stand with feet roughly shoulder-width apart with knees slightly bent for balance.

Standing bicep curls

Technique: In the standing position, keep the elbows against the sides of your body. Hold weights in each hand slightly in front of you, palms facing up and elbows slightly bent. Exhale

as you bring the weights up as far as you can, bringing your hands towards your shoulders. Do not move your elbows away from the body. Hold for a second and then inhale as you slowly bring the hands down to the starting position.

Standing hammer curls

Technique: The technique of hammer curls is similar to the Standing bicep curls. In the starting position, stand with the weights in your hands with palms facing inwards towards your body and keep the palms in the same angle, turned inwards as you raise the hands up towards the shoulders. Like the bicep curl, breathe out when you raise your hands and breathe in when you come back to the starting position.

Keep the elbows slightly bent even when you bring the weights down completely.

Overhead dumb bell presses

Technique: Holding the weights in each hand, raise the hands on either side above your shoulders. The elbows should be at a ninety-degree angle just slightly below your shoulders. This is the starting position. Exhale as you raise your hands up in a straight line. Do not straighten your elbows completely. Keep them just slightly bent when you have raised the hands up fully. Hold that position for a second and then

inhale as you slowly lower your hands to come into the starting position.

Tricep extensions

Technique: To do these double arm tricep extensions, grasp one dumb bell firmly between both hands and hold it behind your head so that your elbows are pointing upwards. This is the starting position. Exhale as you raise the weight as high as you can above your head. Don't lock your elbows completely when you have raised your hands fully. Inhale as you slowly return to the starting position.

Advanced tricep dips with legs up (page 229 to 230)

Pull-ups variation 1 (easy and advanced versions) (page 262 to 263)

Pull-ups variation 2 (easy and advanced versions) (page 264)

Connecting exercise:

Shadow boxing (page 258 to 260)

Leg strengthening

Hold the squat position longer

Technique: In this variation exercise for leg strengthening, do a squat (page 69 to 70) and when you are in the final position of a squat with your knees at a ninety-degree angle, hold that position for as long as you comfortably can. After holding for a few seconds, you will start feeling a good contraction on your quadriceps. Hold this position according to your capacity.

Squats with dumb-bells

Technique: The technique of these squats is very similar to the normal squat (page 69 to 70). Hold the weights in both hands and keep the hands by your sides with elbows just slightly bent. Continue to hold the weights in your hands in that position with the elbows slightly bent as you do squats. The added weight will make the squats more challenging for the leg muscles. Inhale as you go down and exhale as you come up.

Sideways lunges (Easy and advanced versions) (page 256 to 257)

Back strengthening:
Sarpasana (page 98)
Dand push-ups (page 253 to 255)
Connecting exercise:
Cat stretch (page 159 to 150)
Straight punches (page 156 to 157)

Stomach strengthening, Set 1:

On-elbow leg raises (one leg and both legs—easy and advanced versions) (page 104 to 105)

Dynamic toe touching variation 1—challenging version 2 (page 98 to 99)

Reverse crunches

Technique: Lie down on your back with hands behind your neck, your fingers interlocked. Raise your neck up slightly and look up at the ceiling. Raise your feet up with knees slightly bent.

This is the starting position. While breathing out bring your knees towards your forehead, raising the hips up slightly. Pause for a fraction of a second with your hips raised, feeling a crunch on the stomach. Breathe in as you take your hips and knees to the starting position. Do as many as you comfortably can. Do not pull your neck up while doing these.

Hanging leg raises for abs (page 265)

Connecting exercise: Sideways—toe inward—leg raises
Technique: The technique for these is similar to the side leg raises (page 236 to 237). The only difference is that you keep the toes of the leg being raised pointing inward towards the floor in front of you throughout the movement unlike the earlier side leg raises where the toe was pointing up and towards your head when raised. With this leg alignment, you will feel a contraction in your gluteal muscles when you raise the leg up.

Stomach strengthening, Set 2:

Holding the 'On-elbow leg raise'

Technique: Take the position for the 'On-elbow leg raises (page 104 to 105). Hold the position with your legs just six inches above the ground. Hold there for a few seconds or a minute according to your capacity.

Cool Down

Gentle cardio

Gentle spot jogging (page 280)

For the cool down, keep the spot jogging very gentle and slow.

Cool down exercises

Leg up hamstring stretch

Technique: Put your right leg up on a bench or table which is at a comfortable height for you. Reach for your right toe with your right hand while stretching the right toe inwards towards you. Hold the stretch that you will feel on your hamstrings and calf muscles for a few seconds. Repeat with the other leg.

Leg up inner thigh stretch

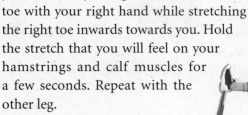

Technique: Put your right leg up like you did for the 'Leg up hamstring stretch'. Now instead of facing your raised leg, turn your body to the left so that the stretched leg is on your right side. Reach for your right toe with your right hand and simultaneously stretch your left hand above your head and towards your

right toe. Hold this final position for a few seconds.
You will feel a stretch on the inner thigh of your
right leg and the left side of the body. Repeat the
same stretch on the other side, this time raising
your left leg.

Leg up calf stretch

Technique: Place toes of your right
foot on the edge of a step or any other
comfortable height. Push
the heel of your right
leg down gently till you
feel a stretch on your calf
muscles. Hold the stretch
for a few seconds and then repeat with the other leg.

Relaxation

Setubandhasana (Bridge posture) (page 166 to 167)
Makarasana (Crocodile posture) Variation 1
(page 58)
Makarasana (Crocodile posture)
Variation 2 (page 58)
Sukhasana (Stretching
body tall) (page 89 to
90)
Breath awareness with
hands on stomach (page
106)

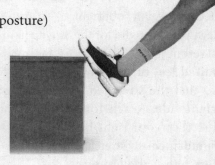

A 20-Minute Session with Deepika Padukone

When I was in boarding school at Scindia, I was a big fan of Deepika's father—the legendary badminton player Prakash Padukone. While I played many different sports at school, badminton was not one of them. The only exposure I had to badminton was during the vacations, when I religiously watched episodes of a sports programme on national television in which Prakash Padukone gave tips on the sport. The moment the programme finished, I would practise what he'd just taught on the show. Little did I know that all that practice would help me several years later when I would train his daughter in fitness!

It was a memorable day for me when Prakash Padukone, the former World No. 1, gifted me a badminton racket. I had just finished a session with Deepika and her mom, who was visiting her at the time, when the bell rang. Prakash had come straight from the airport with his suitcase in one hand and a brand new professional badminton racket in the other. He had carried that as a gift for me to acknowledge my contribution to his daughter and wife's fitness. I had been training Ujjwala Padukone, Deepika's mom, only for brief periods during her visits to Mumbai. Though she was already quite fit and regular with her workouts back in Bengaluru, I introduced a few new elements in her routine which made a very positive difference to her fitness.

When Deepika called me for the first time to tell me she wanted to train with me, she suggested we start at 5:30 the next morning. I reconfirmed, wondering if I'd heard right. 'Are you sure you want to workout at 5.30 am?' 'Yes, absolutely!' she replied enthusiastically.

I had trained many people from the film industry and most of them never wanted to work out so early. Most actors I'd encountered usually woke up late, unless they had an early morning shoot. To my pleasant surprise, the next morning Deepika was ready for the workout at the appointed time.

Though we now work out around 6 am on most days, there have been times when she has had to leave for a very early shoot and we've worked out as early as 4.30 am! I must admit, even if I'm late once in a while, but she's always ready on time. I think it has something to do with the discipline of being a sportsperson herself and being the daughter of a great sportsman.

Deepika's building has a nice garden, a ground, a terrace, and a very steep slope going up to the main gate. We constantly make use of all of them for our workouts. Many times when we work out very early in the morning, we go running on the roads outside as part of our warm up.

Though Deepika and I usually work out for 45 minutes to an hour—I'm giving you an example of her 20-minute workout, when she's had a late-night shoot and has to report early in the morning on set.

Once in a while, when we do a fuller session, we do the entire workout in the garden itself. We sometimes play a game of badminton as a warm up to break the monotony of our usual warm up. Not surprisingly, she is a fantastic player. Her dad's tips, which I'd picked up as a teenager, and my sports background just about help me give her a tough fight. I tell her that the reason she wins against me, even without running around too much, is because she has such long limbs! We generally end these sessions by walking barefoot on the grass.

In a short session like this one, we don't do the cartwheels, handstands, or short sprints that we sometimes include in the longer workouts in the garden.

I reach her place at 6.30 am and she's ready with her shoes on. Her house is on the seventh floor and we always walk down the seven floors of her building.

- We go to the garden and start with an easy walk. While walking, we take a few deep breaths. At that time of the morning, just being outdoors in the midst of greenery and breathing in fresh air is tremendously energizing.
- After a minute of easy walking, we increase the pace and start brisk walking. This is the 'Heating Up the Body 1' (page 76) section of the warm up.
- After a couple of minutes of brisk walking, we stop and do the 'Warm up Exercises 1' (page 76 to 78) to stimulate the joints and muscles. We do these stretches in the part of the

garden which has direct sunlight, so she can get the fantastic benefits of the morning sun as well.

- After stretches, we jog on the grass for 2 to 3 minutes. This is the 'Heating Up the Body 2' (page 79) section of the warm up.
- We then stop to do the 'Warm up Exercises 2' (page 79 to 86), to further warm up the body.
- Next, starting our main workout, we do a few push-ups, followed by the Hamstring stretch using a small boundary wall of the garden (page 297).
- Following that, we practise a few martial arts kicks. After the kicks, we practise a few tricep dips using the bench in her garden. (page 132 to 133).

For her strength training, we mostly practise freehand movements like push-ups and squats, which use her own body weight. These work on several muscle groups at the same time, including the core muscles. This kind of freehand training prepares the body for functional fitness. Another person might achieve a similar muscle tone by doing exercises that isolate different muscles. Even though that kind of training is more time consuming, when it comes to actual performance of any kind such as playing a sport or rock climbing, the person who practises more freehand techniques will have an edge.

Many people tell me, 'Oh, you train Deepika, she is so thin and toned!' I tell them that more importantly, she is truly fit.

Being thin and looking toned are the pleasant side effects of the athletic workouts she does and her healthy diet. There are many people who may look thin and toned but are not fit. In her case, through her freehand workouts and yoga practice, she maintains true athletic functional fitness and a centred mind. She is as comfortable sprinting really fast as she is sitting still in meditation for a considerable amount of time.

- We do some skipping (page 261) and shuffling movements in the garden itself. These movements encourage you to be light on your feet. Being light on the feet is really important for a sportsperson and also for anyone who wants to feel light and become light.

- After doing the skipping and shuffling movements for a minute, we run up the seven flights of stairs to her home, as fast as possible. I pay special attention that we make minimum sound while being light on our feet.

- By the time she reaches the door, her heart is beating fast and the breathing rate has also gone up considerably. This last leg of our intensive cardio will make sure that her metabolic rate stays high through the day, burning calories more efficiently for many hours even after the workout.

- Inside in her living room, which overlooks the sea, the large window is left open to let in the fresh air. The fan is switched off and her yoga mat is placed in the centre.

- I make her do the standing quadriceps stretch ('Bending knee back with support', page 77), which helps to relax these muscles after the running up the stairs.

- She has a few sips of room temperature water before she sits on the mat to do the stretches to loosen up her leg muscles, which have been extensively used so far ('Sitting— both legs in front toe touching', page 125 to 126).

- She then does the wake-up stretches for the spine ('Wake-up stretches variation B', page 177 to 179).

- This is followed by standing postures (Vrikshasana, page 87 and Tadasana, page 122) and then six cycles of the Suryanamaskar. She does the six cycles of Suryanamaskar slowly and gracefully. Her breathing and movement are completely coordinated. When she finishes the six cycles, her breathing rate is not fast. Some days we do more cycles of Suryanamaskar and some days less. On most days we incorporate nine to twelve cycles.

- After doing the Suryanamaskar, she lies down on her back for a few seconds, just watching her breath—feeling the enhanced energy flow in the body ('Breath awareness with hands on the stomach', page 106).

- I then make her practise the Setubandhasana (page 166 to 167), which relaxes the spine, followed by the Spinal twist, (page 148 to 149) and Pavanmuktasana (page 60).

- This is followed by the lying down dynamic Paschimottanasana (Dynamic toe touching variation 1) six times.

- We then move onto 'Side leg raises' (page 236 to 237).

- Then turn over onto the stomach for back strengthening postures ('Back strengthening variations 1 and 2'), (page 67 to 68).

- Then on her back again for 'Stomach strengthening exercises', 'Hands behind the neck leg raises' (page 163 to 164), and 'Crunches' (page 165).

- As a counter-stretch to the stomach exercises, I make her do a Chakrasana (page 251).

- Chakrasana is followed by the Sarvangasana (page 249). Here we do a Pavanmuktasana (page 60) again to relax the spine.

- Before moving onto the relaxation part of the session, I ask Deepika to stretch her spine and body tall ('Lying-down body stretch', page 150).
- I take her into a Shavasana, relaxing the whole body, focusing on the breathing. Since this is a short workout day, we do the Shavasana for only about a minute. I ask her to take her time to roll over onto one side and get into a sitting posture. She sits still in Vajrasana (page 92), with her mind centred for a few seconds. We follow this up with some deep breathing.
- She ends the session by putting her head to the floor in a variation of Shashankasana (page 96).

Sure enough, by the time we end, we've overshot the 20 minutes! As I leave, she thanks me with a big smile as she gets ready to start another busy day feeling fit, centred, and full of energy.

Conclusion

I have had the good fortune of being able to help a lot of people I have trained over the years, including many celebrities, to enhance their quality of life and productivity through the very methods described in this book. Through the book, I have shown you the same systematic, healthy, and holistic way to take charge of your fitness.

But what I can't do for the people I train is give them their motivation. They bring that with them to the workout sessions. I would expect the same of you.

If you do not take care of your holistic fitness, you will not only be compromising on the quality and productivity of your life but will also be heading towards several health problems, which can easily be avoided by regular exercise. Just like smoking is an abuse to your health and well-being, so is leading a sedentary lifestyle.

You have made a start by investing in this book. You have come on a journey with me because of your personal motivation to get fit and stay fit, for life. As you get better at the exercises, and fitter, you'll enjoy your workouts much more.

However, no matter how motivated you are, there will be phases in your life when you won't be able to follow your workout routine regularly. And that is absolutely fine as long as you keep getting back to it each time. Make sure to start at an easier intensity whenever there is a long gap. You can even start with the 'One-Month Commitment' all over again. Keep dipping into this book like a manual—there is a lot of valuable information in it.

Even when you are going through days when you are not being able to follow your workout routine, do not let yourself slide back completely. Make sure you at least do your 'Wake-up stretches' and stay active throughout the day.

It is absolutely fine if you were moving house or travelling so you could not manage your workout routine for two weeks but what is not fine is that you were absolutely inactive for those two weeks. As long as you keep yourself active and manage whatever little exercise you can on such days, it will be easy for you to return to your proper routine.

At least twenty minutes of physical activity in the whole day is the bare minimum. Walking to your car at a leisurely pace does not count, taking the stairs and brisk walking does.

Even on busier days when you do not have a workout scheduled, make sure to squeeze in a little exercise. I find a few minutes before jumping into the shower in the morning a great time to do this and get it out of the way. Whatever more you can do in the rest of the day in terms of brisk walking and taking the stairs will be a bonus.

If you haven't been able to do sufficient physical activity through the day, it's important to get your heart racing and your muscles contracted and stretched a bit before you eat dinner. In case you are already quite hungry, then eat first and after an hour or so, go for a gentle walk. Don't let the fact that you have eaten dinner be an excuse to skip the gentle walk!

No matter what, at the end of the day, ask yourself:

Did I get some Exercise Today?

And if the answer is NO, then step out now. Even a twenty minute walk will be a good start.

No matter how 'busy' or 'lazy' you are, if you do not take charge of your fitness in a holistic manner then you are doing a big disservice to yourself and your loved ones, and severely compromising on the quality of your life. You are taking yourself closer to premature ageing, heart problems, diabetes and cancer which are not fun at all. They can very much happen to you and me.

Believe me, it's just the initial bit of pulling yourself out of bed and first few days of workouts and lifestyle changes that are tough but once you tide over that and make the fitness routine a part of your life, you will always thank yourself later for making that initial effort.

And don't buy into shortcuts; you will only be short-changing yourself. Walking on the treadmill while watching TV, and drinking a packaged fruit juice that is nice on your taste buds, is not going to get you anywhere. Go brisk walking and jogging outdoors in the fresh air and bite into a real fruit.

My yoga Guruji, Dr Hansraj Yadav, often shares his simple mantra for being healthy and in turn happy in life. He says the key is to keep '*pair garam, pet naram aur sar thandaa*' , literally translated—'Feet warm, stomach soft and head cool' and meaning:

a) Use your feet a lot—move, walk and be active.
b) Eat wholesome food which aids good digestion.
c) Keep your mind calm and relaxed.

Holistic fitness taken up in the correct way does take effort initially but there comes a point where it becomes effortless and pure bliss.

Through this book, I have tried to share with you the precious 'fitness gems' that I have received from my teachers in a simple and easy to follow format. I hope it will help you enhance your own 'healthy glow' and spread it to others around you as well.

Chart for the One-Month Commitment (Chapter 4)

Days:	Week One	Week Two	Week Three	Week Four
Monday				
Tuesday				
Wednesday				
Thursday				
Friday				
Saturday				
Sunday				

Acknowledgements

I would like to thank some key people who inspired me, helped shape my vision, and without whom this book would not have been possible.

Pia Sukanya, for lending me her ear and offering her unwavering confidence and belief in what I do. She was my sounding board, the first one to read whatever I wrote, and was present at every step—fighting with me with all her passion and gusto to make this a better book. She helped me give shape to my rough notes and has been the greatest support during the journey of writing this book.

My editor at Random House India, Milee Ashwarya, for her patience, and persistent encouragement. I am grateful for her valuable inputs and for being so receptive to my ideas. If not for her perseverance, it would have taken an eternity for me to finish my first draft. The entire Random House India team, who believed in my work, and put in great effort to give the best shape to my ideas in the form of this book.

Deepika Padukone, for her invaluable support. She is always an inspiration. One of the best examples of true holistic fitness—her sincerity, discipline, dedication, and that ever-bright smile are truly motivating.

Ranbir Kapoor for his immense belief in me and for inspiring me.

Michael Ward regularly lent me his abundant enthusiasm, which I so needed in writing this book. I have incorporated many of his brilliant suggestions and am incredibly grateful for his constant guidance and support.

Swara Bhaskar, for agreeing to read my manuscript at different stages and giving very valuable inputs. I hope she will incorporate at least some of the 'healthy habits' that I have mentioned in the book.

My students and clients inspire me with their commitment, unconditional love, and respect. I thank them for being extremely considerate and self-motivated while I isolated myself in order to complete this book.

A big thanks to Shivang, Nishtha, Manish Rachoya, Hema, Tanu Bhargava, Piyush, Jyoti Gidwani, Neha Sareen, Sunil Bhatia, Ranimol T.A., Dheera Kitchlu, Ektaa Malik, Dhirendra Tiwari, Darshan Jalan, Pooja Pradhan, Indra Sharma, Sunita Kapoor, Priya Chandrasekar, Anku Pande, and my aunt Suman Sharma for their contribution to make this a better book.

Alvira Khan Agnihotri for her rock-solid support and encouragement.

Yogacharya Dr Hansaraj Yadav for greatly enhancing my understanding and practice of yoga.

Mr Thakur, who was the yoga teacher at my school, for sharing his knowledge and encouraging me to follow a career in holistic fitness.

Dr Karan Singh for encouraging me and inspiring me to maximize my potential.

'Yogi' Durlabhji, for being a great inspiration and always insisting that I should write a book!

My dearest sister, Uttama, who told me all the things that my book should not be while I was still writing the initial outline. I have tried my best to match up to her expectations!

Raja, my adorable dog, for being by my side while I sat working on the book through the nights and boosting my creativity by forcing me to take the useful breaks at regular intervals to play with him.

And finally my parents, my ultimate inspiration, who have always urged me to follow my passion. They are the real reason this book exists.

A Note on the Author

Abhishek Sharma was born in Jaipur and educated at the Scindia School, Gwalior and St. Stephen's College, Delhi. He is a much-sought-after celebrity fitness coach and holistic trainer, now based in Mumbai. Over the past ten years, he has trained Deepika Padukone, Ranbir Kapoor, Anil Kapoor, Subrata Roy

Sahara, Akshaye Khanna, Sonam Kapoor, and Sarah Jane Dias among many others. In his holistic workout sessions, Abhishek combines elements from classical yoga, martial arts, and freehand athletic workouts to enhance the fitness and well-being of the people he trains.

Abhishek is a rare combination of a martial artist, athlete, as well as being an exponent of classical yoga. Taking elements from all these disciplines, he has evolved a holistic workout practice he calls *Victory Yoga*. This practice is meant for the modern day Arjuna, who needs to face challenges and realise his/her true potential. The workout is designed to help develop both a truly fit body and a centred mind.

Abhishek also moonlights as a photographer, and has clicked many of the photographs in this book.

www.victoryoga.com

During the shooting of a film in Himachal Pradesh where I was training actors Deepika Padukone, Ranbir Kapoor, Kalki Koechlin, and Aditya Roy Kapoor. I took them outdoors on their day off. We trekked to a beautiful, remote village and had an incredible experience.

Deepika and Aditya at the beginning of the trek in chilly weather.

Deepika dodging branches of an apple tree and crossing one of the several streams we encountered along the way.

Deepika sitting on a rock in a mustard field.

Kalki climbs mountains effortlessly, as she has accompanied her father, an avid mountaineer on many treks. We came across a waterfall and she decided to take a dip in the ice cold water.

After that brief halt at the waterfall, on our journey overlooking the snow peaks.

On reaching the village we were showered with true Himachali warmth and hospitality, served local organic food, and each one of us was gifted a traditional cap and muffler.

Deepika surrounded by village kids.

The village elder and our host Meher Chand ji seeing us off as the villagers look on excitedly.

After a run on the highway towards Rohtang pass. It was dark and extremely cold and we were carrying one big torch as we ran uphill for several kilometres. After the run, we came back indoors and I made the group do a lot of stretches to relax the muscles. This picture of Ranbir, Deepika, Kalki, Aditya, and me was clicked by Mehera, Deepika's make-up artist.

Sessions with Miss India contestants. In their training, I included a lot of stretches and breathing exercises to help them be calm and relaxed and also many back bending yoga poses to improve their posture.

Actor Darshan Jariwala who played Mahatma Gandhi in Gandhi, My Father. I made him run as if for a marathon to lose weight and do a lot of breathing and meditation to look and feel like his on-screen character.

Running at the Marine Drive promenade—one of my favourite places to run in Mumbai.

After finishing a ten kilometre run at Marine Drive on a Sunday morning. Many times we've enjoyed running in the rain!

With my group after a game of basketball.

At our starting point at 7 am. Sunday mornings are best for cycling as the traffic is less.

At around 10:30 am, we reach our finishing point which is a popular breakfast joint. All of us really look forward to our well deserved scrambled eggs and some other high calorie snacks. Such foods are absolutely fine once in a while as long as you are active enough.

Wall climbing which is almost like rock climbing is a great way to test your functional fitness. This is the first time I took my group for a fun, challenging activity which requires a good level of fitness, specially core strength.